ANGLING

in the

SHADOWS

of the

CANADIAN
ROCKIES

*A complete guide to fishing in
southern British Columbia & Alberta*

*Compiled and Edited
by
Jeff Mironuck*

Flies for Angling in the Shadows of the Canadian Rockies can be purchased through Jeff Mironuck at 250-489-4908, or e-mail: jeffmironuck@hotmail.com.

Distributed by **Gordon Soules Book Publishers Ltd.**
1359 Ambleside Lane, West Vancouver, BC Canada V7T 2Y9
PMB 620, 1916 Pike Place #12, Seattle,WA 98101-1097, US
604-922-6588 Fax: 604-688-5442 E-mail: books@gordonsoules.com
Web site: http://www.gordonsoules.com

Canadian Cataloguing in Publication Data

Mironuck, Jeff, 1977 -
    Angling in the Shadows of the Canadian Rockies

    ISBN 0-9683955-1-1

    1. Fishing--Canada, Western. 2. Fly fishing--Canada, Western. I. Title.
SH571.M62 1999   799.1'2'09712   C99-910721-6

Front cover photo by David Lambroughton
Back cover photo by Jeff Mironuck

Angling in the Shadows of the Canadian Rockies

ISBN 0-9683955-1-1

Second Edition 1999
Printed in Canada
Copyright 1999 by Jeff Mironuck

Acknowledgments

I could not have covered such a large area without the help of so many individuals. Steve Harris, Gerry Frederick, Brian Oke, Matt Palmer and Pete Morrison are some of the best anglers I've fished with and over the period of compiling this book they gave me many ideas and suggestions. Paul Augustine and Randy Martin from Mountain Man in Cranbrook answered many of my questions and gave their opinions as well. My parents allowed me to turn the basement into a mess of information and photos. I appreciated their patience and help. Anglers from around the regions gave me the information and photos I needed. Kootenay Kwik Print once again put up with my constant questions. Anyone who has gone through this knows how important good publishers can be. Kendra Konkin and Alan Doddy came up with some great sketches. Both of them are quality artists. When I was stuck for a name, Bev Hills helped me out with the title. Many others, which are just to numerous to name, have each contributed something to this book. I thank everyone for without all the support I received I couldn't have finished it.

Foreword

Fly fishing has become increasingly popular over the last few years. With more of the general population having extra time for recreational activities the waters are frequented often. Many years ago killing the entire catch was normal. Even today I'm asked "why catch them if you can't eat them?". My general response to this is "If everyone kept all their catch, there would simply be no more fish to catch in the future!" It's important that people realize the condition of our precious resource. Fly fishing teaches us the values of life. I have seen many friendships built on the stream. Most fly fishers I know seem to have a great respect for their environment. Catch and release and fly fishing seem to go hand in hand. I enjoy teaching others how to fly fish in hopes that they will come to enjoy the sport for more than just dinner. We look at God's creations, the beauty of a rainbow or the willingness of a cutthroat. They were all created for us to enjoy. If we are careful with them they will be there for us for many more angling seasons.

Yes, it's true one person could have written a book on fly fishing south western Canada. I don't believe the book would have been complete. New waters bring new challenges and there is always something special about fishing in them. I remember the first time I had fished the Crowsnest. After reading articles and hearing the stories of the wild rainbows, visions of dry flies and crystal waters were painted in my head before I even cast a line out. My first step into the water opened a new door with many new challenges and experiences to come.

I could have written on the spectacular lakes of the interior or perhaps the diverse stillwaters of southern Alberta, however, would you not want to read an article from someone who's only fished there a few times. I know the water around my home just as others know their water. From steelheading the Cowichan to tackling rainbows on the Bow, this book brings together many different writers that share some of their techniques and thoughts. I owe them all a special thanks. I hope everyone will enjoy this book and if it helps you catch a few extra fish just remember to release them.

Dedicated to my parents
and all fishers who release fish.
And to God for allowing us to marvel at
some of his beautiful creations in his
astounding environment.

Kendra Konkin

Table of Contents

Entomology and Food Source Profiles of South Western Canada

In our small corner of the world we are blessed with some of the best fishing available to anglers. From the weeded bottom lakes of B.C. to the nutrient rich waters of the Bow River in Alberta, fish have ample food sources to thrive. There are many food sources that are commonly found throughout south western Canada. I will try to fill you in on what these are and how the fisherman can imitate them at the appropriate time.

Freshwater Shrimp

Commonly found in many lakes and some streams, these small scuds are available to the fish throughout the angling year. The Gammarus shrimp is larger in size than the Hyalella shrimp and is also more predominant. Gammarus prefer environments with high levels of calcium. Gammarus are generally found in sizes between 10 and 30 mm. Often these scuds are found in colors such as olives and pinks. Gammarus body color will take on the color of its surrounding in most situations. Many anglers neglect the use of scud imitations. This is often a mistake as the scuds represent a staple food for fish. The Baggy Shrimp is a favorite of many anglers due to its easy tying requirements. Long winter months cause trout in lakes to focus in on scuds as other food items become scarce. Scuds are also responsible for the beautiful pink stripe found on many rainbows. Hyalella are harder for anglers to imitate due to their size. They are generally found in sizes between 2 and 5 mm. Hyalella can adapt better to their surrounding and are found in many alpine lakes. All scuds prefer water with good weed cover. Fish can often be seen along the shoal trying to dig out scuds with their noses. Scuds are not fast swimmers but they do create attention with their short drops and twisting actions. Early spring and fall are the best time to fish scuds.

Chironomid

This is one of the most challenging aspects of stillwater angling and at the same time it can be the most enjoyable experience. I myself, find great satisfaction in "matching the hatch". There are thousands of species of chironomids but only a handful of colors and sizes. Most anglers should carry them in sizes of 22 to 6 and colors of brown, red, maroon, black and many shades of green. This is by no means a complete list. All waters vary to a certain degree and almost every color imaginable can be found. Chironomids go through a complete life cycle where in every stage they are food for fish.

The larvae, pupae and adults can all be imitated by the angler. Most chironomid larvae are red in color due to the fluids in their bodies. This fluid which is similar to hemoglobin is extremely bright and attracts fish. Bloodworms as they are generally called move in a wiggling motion when not lying on the lake bottom. Storms or heavy winds can cause them to be swept off the bottom where fish can gorge themselves. I enjoy fishing these and feel that the larger fish in a lake will key in on these at certain times. The larvae will live in mud tubes and at the right time they will seal themselves inside and begin their transformation to the pupal stage.

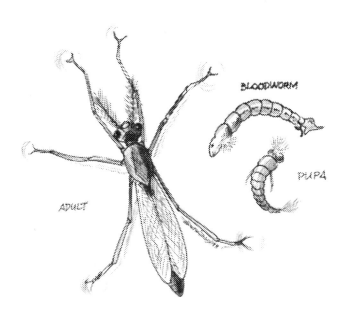

After this transformation is completed, the pupae breaks from the tube and slowly begins its vertical ascent to the surface. This emergence can cause trout to feed on nothing else. This is also what brings frustration to many anglers. Large trout have to feed on huge numbers of these pupas due to their small size. The pupae ascent can be imitated by using a floating line and a long leader which could allow the fly to sink within a foot of the bottom. A slow re-trieve can work well and just allowing the fly to remain still can also be effective. When the pupae reaches the surface, the back of the thorax splits and the adult emerges onto the surface and shortly there-after flies off to mate. The adult stage can be represented with dries such as a Tom Thumb. Although chironomid fishing can seem very difficult, there are some things you can look for which will increase you odds. Watch for swallows and other birds skimming the sur-faces. These birds are often feeding on the adults, but they will at least tell you where the fish are feeding and you will also know that chironomids are emerging. Looking on the water for emerging chi-ronomids could tell you what color and size to try if you see one. Using a stomach pump and pumping the first fish caught can show you the last few food items taken. Watching for these signs will increase your success.

Damsel flies

Hard takes and broken line can be associated with fishing the damsel. In the nymph stage the damsels can be found in a similar habitat to the shrimp. They are an important food source to the fish, especially when in their emergence swim. I prefer to fish these during their emergence as that can bring on the most explosive strikes. Short pulls with frequent rests can produce good results. On their emergence they are commonly found near the surface making their way to bulrush stems or lily pads. Occasionally you will be lucky enough to see a large fish cruising through the bulrushes trying to knock the emerging damsels into the water. At this time I fish them close to the edge or in the bulrushes. Patterns tied with marabou are most effective in sizes 8 through 12.

In the adult stage the damsel looks like a thin dragonfly. Blue or brown adults can be found and patterns of deer hair or foam are commonly used. Brook trout will chase these flies more than any other fish I can think of. I always keep a couple in my box.

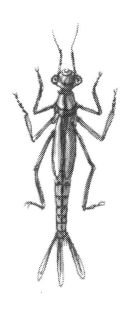

Dragonflies

Gomphus and Darners can live up to 4 years in the nymph stage and are a large meal for fish. Although mainly found in stillwater, some can be found in slow moving streams. Similar to damsels, the dragons migrate to the shoreline to emerge only once in their life. Gomphus and Darners are very different and have to be fished accordingly. Gomphus prefer to lay in wait for their prey. Crawling on the bottom appeals to them more than swimming. They reach sizes upwards of 3 inches in some cases although 1 to 2 inches are more common. Darners are good swimmers and seek mayfly nymphs and scuds for food. They are very fast and can even catch minnows at times. I fish one pattern for both types and then vary the way I retrieve depending on what type the fish are taking. Patters tied with chenille, marabou, deer hair and foam will all work. Darners can be fished with slow pulls and quick jerks while the Gomphus should be fished on the bottom in a slow steady motion. May, June and July are the best times to fish these as its the major emergence period for the fully developed nymphs. At this time, I like to anchor in shallow water and pull the nymph along the drop-off and onto the shoal. Adults are occasionally taken when they land on the water.

Mayflies

Most anglers think of streams when talking about mayflies. A simple cycle to follow with only the nymphs and adults offered to the fish. In the river these nymphs can be seen clinging to rocks or scurrying over them. Occasionally they become dislodged where they drift down stream to an eager trout. They are common in the spring right through late fall. Moist days and low light periods seem to bring out the larger hatches in most of my experiences. The Callibaetis is the most abundant species found in our waters. On the stream, mayflies are found hatching close to the surface in the slower water. They are available to trout on their emergence swim and fishing them with a dead drift or short pulls will produce. Dead drifting with a indicator on most streams is the most effective way I've found to fish these nymphs. High-sticking them works well when the fish are in close. Pete Morrison demonstrates the proper technique on page 25 of this book. The adult is one of the most delicate dries that an angler can fish. Duns are dull in color and the spinners are very shiny. The spinners emerge once the duns shed their outer skin. Both adults hold their wings in an upright position which make them very visible to trout and anglers alike.

On the lakes the matured nymphs swim to the surface and emerge. This motion can be imitated with slow long pulls and quick short jerks. Pauses are very important as skeptical trout may follow for quite awhile before taking the imitation. I like to vary my retrieve and a Pheasant Tail or a Mironymph are good patterns. Dry fly fishing and mayflies often go hand in hand. They are one of the easiest dries to imitate and fish. I like to use almost any dun pattern that matches the hatch. Adam's in various sizes imitate the dun well and can also be used for searching waters. Blue Green Olives work excellent when fishing mayflies in the spent position.

Caddis flies

Caddis flies, also known as sedges, have a complete metamorphosis with all stages being fed on by fish. The larva cases are formed by surrounding debris using sand, pebbles, sticks or whatever is available. This larvae stage usually lasts between 1 and 2 years in both streams and lakes. Larvae that do build cases have to build new ones as they grow in size. At the proper time they seal themselves inside and become fully developed pupa. After breaking free the pupa uses its powerful legs to swim to the surface to emerge. This stage can bring some excellent opportunities for fly fishers. Many patterns are available. I like to use a type 3 full sink and pull the fly in using a varied retrieve with many different speeds. The same technique will work well on most stream. Only seconds after reaching the surface the pupa emerges, dries its wings and prepares for flight. These tent shaped insects attract a lot of attention as flying off the surface is quite a challenge. June, July and August are prime times for caddis fishing. On streams I prefer the Elk Hair Caddis while the Tom Thumb remains a classic and my personal favorite on the lakes.

Many articles have been written on what a sedge hatch can do to trout. I'm not sure if they taste better, maybe a few less bones than a dragonfly. Trout attack these flies like their last meal is getting away. When fishing the caddis I prefer a strong leader with at least 5 lb. tippet. Skittering your pattern with 3 or 4 short pulls followed by a rest is a good method on the lakes, while a dead drift and moderate action is the key on the streams.

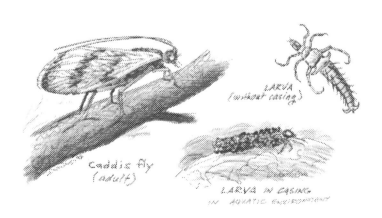

LARVA
(without casing)

Caddis fly
(adult)

LARVA IN CASING
IN AQUATIC ENVIRONMENT

Water Boatman

The boatman is carefully watched by many successful fly fishers. These fast swimming beetle like insects are best fished in the early spring and late fall. Long legs help propel them at good speeds. Unlike the similar backswimmer which swims on its back, the water boatman swims with dips and dives on its stomach using oxygen captured at the surface. Eggs to the fully formed winged adult takes about 1 year to complete. Patterns tied with foam and rubber legs work great as you can fish it with a sinking line, pausing periodically to allow the boatmen to float to the surface. I've found that trout will take this fly at anytime of the retrieve. Fishing it along the weed line after a good frost in the fall or early spring will ensure good success with it.

A nice trout taken on a Water Boatman

Leeches

A great fly for any beginner on lakes. Leeches are primarily found on the bottom in all zones of a lake. Occasionally they will be sighted on the surface after being scooped up by waves or a good storm. As with dragonflies, leeches are an available food item throughout the year. Coming in various sizes and different shades of green, brown and black they swim in a snakelike movement. Big fish like them and I can't think of one particular pattern that brings in more large fish. Patterns tied with marabou have that real life movement, I try to carry as many different shades and sizes as possible. Trolling leeches is always productive although many prefer stripping them with sinking lines at various speeds. Night fishing with long, large leeches on the shoal of a lake can be fantastic. In mid summer trout move onto the cool shoals at night to feed. Long casts with quick jerky retrieves will prove effective. I like patterns such as various Marabou Leeches and Flashy Woolly Buggers.

Stone flies

Large and small stone flies hatch at various times throughout the season in our streams. They can create great nymphing and some excellent dry fly fishing after they finish emerging. Many streams are filled with small stones like the Elk River and yet some streams like the Crowsnest are famous for the larger stones. I always look under rocks for any signs of the nymphs. Stone flies offer the angler a great pattern to use even for searching some water on a slower day. Nymphs are found in many colors ranging from black and brown to yellow. While moving from the deeper stretches of the stream to edges they are picked off by searching trout. After crawling onto rocks out of the water the nymph breaks free and emerges into the full adult. These adults are taken greedily on top by trout and patterns such as Tom Thumbs, Sofa Pillows and Stimulators should all work. I've found them to be a valuable pattern that must be kept in the box at all times.

Large brook trout taken on a stone fly nymph

Game Fish of South Western Canada

Rainbow Trout

The most sought after fish in our waters. The rainbow can be identified by their black spots and the shade of pink that runs the length of their body. In some waters Gerrard rainbows will be found and in other waters the Kamloops rainbow will be more predominate. In the last few years new strains such as the Blackwater rainbows have been successfully introduced to some of our lakes. These trout can adapt better to warmer conditions and like to feed on shiners. Gerrards and Blackwater tend to be more brightly colored than the silvery Kamloops strain. All these rainbows love to jump when hooked and are the best fighting trout around.

The interior of B.C. has become famous for its hard-fighting and high-jumping silvery rainbows that reside in the majority of the lakes there. Rainbows spawn in the spring and take on a darker look. During this time the trout can often be seen cruising the shallows or in spawning channels. At this time these trout should not be disturbed. The rainbow is the most widely distributed fish in south western Canada. Thousands of lakes in B.C. and Alberta are stocked annually with them. Rivers such as the Bow, Oldman and Crowsnest in Alberta along with the Babine, Bulkley, Columbia are just a few of the trophy waters containing good numbers of these trout. The fly fisher has a great advantage over "hardware" anglers when fishing for rainbows due to their tendency towards feeding on insects. Although they may be more selective feeders than other trout, a challenge always makes the catch better.

Cutthroat Trout

Cutthroat come in two main strains, the Westslope and Yellowstone. They are found throughout our waters in many lakes and streams. Cutthroats can be distinguished by red slashes under their jaw, hence their name. Not known for their smartness these trout will often charge aggressively after almost anything that an angler presents to them. This attribute can be great for the beginner but leaves out some of the challenge for the experienced fly fisher. Native to many waters in south western Canada, cutthroat prefer perfect water conditions which much of our area can offer. These trout can get to good sizes and in catch and release areas you will get some of the best hard-pulling, deep-diving trout fighting available. Water such as the Elk River in B.C. and countless alpine lakes will ensure the survival of these trout for a long time.

Brown Trout

Rarely found in most of B.C., brown trout tend to do well in many of Alberta's streams. They are able to share habitat with other trout like rainbows and brookies. The Bow River holds great numbers of different fish species and brown trout thrive there. Brown trout have black, as well as an orange or red spot coloration painted on a light golden brown body. The story of how the Bow River became stocked with brown trout is a good one. In the early 1920's a fisheries truck broke down near the Bow. Instead of letting the fish die, the brown trout were released into the river where to this day they coexist with many other species. Many anglers feel that they are harder to catch than even rainbows. Since these trout can grow to great sizes, they are prized by many fly fishers all over the world.

Brook Trout

I consider the brook trout the most beautiful fish ever angled for. As a member of the char family brookies have olive wormlike markings over their backs and white-tipped fins. Brook trout are not native to our waters and tend not to grow to large sizes on the streams. Brookies can be found in countless creeks and beaver dams throughout both Alberta and B.C. Stocking brook trout in lakes has had some good success. Many lakes now hold trophy trout up to 10 lbs with a good sized brookie weighing about 3 lbs.

Whitefish

Praised by few, these scaly fish are abundant and easy to catch in most streams. Whitefish are generally very tasty and some anglers fish for them exclusively all year. Nymphs work well in areas of fast moving water. Pale yellow in color with a mouth similar to squaw fish, you will find the majority of them near the bottom. Average size is about 12 inches with many streams carrying them to over 20.

Smallmouth and Largemouth Bass

Fly fishers seem to overlook both largemouth and smallmouth bass even with some of the great qualities bass have to offer. Lakes like Duck Lake in B.C. offer the angler bass up to 10 lbs. Many times bass react to being hooked by throwing themselves out of the water followed by long hard dives. Although bass will never get the attention that a trout or salmon attracts, it is still a great game fish which can be caught on a fly rod.

Pike

Found in parts of B.C. and many areas of Alberta, the pike can reach enormous sizes that has to get the attention of at least a few anglers. Over the past few years spoons and bait have been replaced with buck tails and streamers by some adventurous angler. Pike have sharp teeth but with steel leaders they can be brought in. Whether angling in the lakes or streams, a pike can add an element of excitement that many trout fishers have never experienced.

Arctic Grayling

With a large dorsal fin, it's hard not to recognize the grayling. The Little Smoky River is a great place to catch this unique fish. Graylings are easily caught on flies and can present a problem when fishing for another species in grayling water. Schools of these fish are often seen sipping the surface and they readily take dries. Nymphs will work well in most streams as well. Most quality grayling fishing will take you up into northern B.C. and the grayling is native in the Peace and Athabasca River systems in Alberta. Grayling are one of the easiest fish to catch on the fly and for the beginner fly fisher there's no better way to learn.

Pacific Salmons

All five species of Pacific salmon offer the fly fisher a great challenge and an exciting fight. Coho is the most popular of the salmon to catch due to its runs and jumping ability equal to that of a similar sized rainbow. Coho average 5 to 10 lbs. in most streams with many between 15 and 20 lbs. caught every season. However in recent years the coho have had huge reductions in returns. The reasons are not quite clear and many fingers are being pointed. One thing we all know for sure is what a tragedy it would be to lose such a valuable resource. Coho are found in many streams both large and small.

The chinook is the largest specie of Pacific salmon with many reaching between 25 and 50 lbs. Chinook are usually only found in the larger rivers such as the Fraser or the Skeena. These large fish are best known for long battles that make fly fishing very hard. They are rough unless you have the proper gear and sometimes when fishing for the smaller Pacific salmon one may accidentally hook into a chinook unprepared. Although the fight may not be as fast paced as a coho, any fish that size is sure to cause some excitement.

Sockeye, pinks and chum are all smaller than the coho and chinook. With the pink being the smallest and generally easily caught on flies. The males take on a large hump and are commonly referred to as "humpbacks". With the average size being 3 to 6 lbs. they still attract many anglers. Sockeyes are slightly larger than the pink and as the fish mature they become bright red in the body with green to blue heads. Both sockeye and pink salmon are rare catches in the open water of the ocean. Chums have become a more popular game fish over the last few years. This is probably due to an increase in fly fishers and a decrease in the Pacific salmon overall. With worn and dull colors these are good sized salmon between 7 and 15 lbs. even though they may not be all that attractive. Chum generally take flies and you should be prepared for a good hard fight with many runs and some great leaps.

Dolly Varden or Bull Trout

Known for snapping at the smaller fish on the end of your line these aggressive members of the char family live in many of our lakes and streams. Capable of reaching sizes of over 30 lbs., they attract all types of anglers that don't get many chances with the Pacific salmons. Dollies, as they are commonly called, are one of my favorite fish to catch in the rivers. They take hold and dart around in pools or hold fast in the strong currents. Although they don't fight as fast and hard as a rainbow or cutthroat, their sheer size makes them a challenging opponent. After several hard years in Alberta they are back on the rise again. With tight regulations Alberta should have good fish for years to come. Most of the best areas are in the catch and release streams where the fish won't go home for dinner. Dollies and bull trout have quite an appetite. They will attack almost anything that comes their way and in the popular streams this has led to over harvesting. If we watch these fish closely their numbers are sure to climb back up again and reward us with some great fishing.

Steelhead

The steelhead is not a separate species of trout. It is a seagoing rainbow. The steelhead will spawn in the streams and the offspring will stay there usually between 1 and 3 years. After this time they will move to the ocean where the real growing begins. After they return to the rivers they can be found in sizes ranging from about 2 to 25 lbs. with larger fish being caught. Steelhead over 10 lbs. are considered good fish while any over 20 lbs. are trophies by most. The silver rockets have the glorious reputation of being the hardest fighting fish in our waters. Two different runs of steelhead are available to anglers in B.C.

The winter-run can begin as early as November in some streams with December and January being fairly common times. The late winter run could be as late as April or even May. Fly fishing for winter steelhead can be very hard. Air and water temperatures drop and the fish become less active. Fishing is generally deep and at the best of times it's a little slow. The end of February and all of March can warm up the temperature just enough to get the fish a little more active. Fishing deep is still the choice of experienced anglers and wading is easier in the warmer water. Even though a painful picture can be painted on winter steelheading the angler willing to tough it out will enjoy the fight of a lifetime.

Summer-run steelhead is what it's all about. Hundreds of stories have been written and steelheading in B.C. has become famous all over. Beginning early spring on smaller streams and mid summer on the larger rivers, many of these well known runs now take place on classified waters. These classified waters include great rivers such as the Thompson and the Dean. Because of the great conditions this time of the year the fish become very active. They will take flies near the surface and even move great distances to attack flies. High jumps and long hard runs that can loosen screws in any reel are common. Many fish are 5-10 lbs. with the occasional monster over 20 lbs. This is one experience that every angler should get to experience at least once.

A nice winter steelhead

Where, When and How to Fly Fish in Lakes and Streams

So often anglers rush to the water and begin to fish while not really having a clue where to start. Getting the fly in the water as fast as possible is not the answer unless you are extremely familiar with it. Turning over a few rocks or even just looking into the water for likely holding places will increase your angling success. In the next few pages I hope to show you more strategies for both moving and stillwater while explaining where the fish should be.

In streams, where the fish should be and where they are can change in seconds. There are two main functions trout have in moving water. They feed and they rest. Feeding water can be the same as resting water however, often these two situations can be completely different. It's important to remember that even when the trout are resting they will still feed if the fly is presented properly.

Resting water is generally slower and full of cover. A long deep pool with cover such as a few logs of even broken surface water is adequate. Broken water can give trout a feeling of security because their vision is limited and they have difficulty seeing predators, including anglers. Large rocks can create "quiet water" behind them that is very attractive to fish while both feeding and resting. Insects can be swept around the rock into the quiet water for the waiting trout. One of the best methods for getting behind these rocks and into the deeper pools is called "high-stick nymphing." On the following page, Pete Morrison shows exactly how to do it with great success. Weighted flies are a must when using this method. Streamers are also very effective when fishing down deep. Weighted lines and minnow patterns can bring out the largest fish in almost any stream. In some cases, big fish do like big meals. Whether fishing dries, nymphs or streamers it's important to cover all the water. Creating a grid of 1 foot squares will allow you to fish every inch of the water.

Undercut banks can be found in most of our rivers in south western Canada. They are exciting to fish and you should always keep an eye out for them. Terrestrials can fall off the bank into the water and be pushed into the undercut bank. Fish will once again use these banks as resting places and for feeding. Hopper fishing can be deadly when big fish hold on these banks. Tail-outs of pools can be very hard to fish as the fish can easily see you. After fighting and releasing a large fish, the fish needs to rest. Dollies come to

Pete Morrison demonstrating proper
high-stick nymphing

mind anytime I think of big fish on the rivers. Almost every time I release one over 5 pounds, it slides back to the end of the pool in the slow water to rest. When coming up on these fish, long casts and long drifts may be required. Tail-outs are shallow and dry flies can be effective. I like to have at least a 15 foot drift before the fly reaches the fish. You may have to keep the fly in a direct line with the fish as they may not be inclined to move far.

Feeding water can be defined as any water in which fish feed. Riffles and deep runs are common places to find fish searching for food. Watching for any surface activity is crucial. A trout sipping the surface or aggressively attacking a hopper can be a sure sign of feeding activities. It's easy enough to cast a dry in these cases. Anglers tend to forget that in both streams and lakes fish do the majority of feeding under the surface. It's very tough to see a small mayfly being taken, so we must look for the more obvious signs. A stomach pump is a valuable tool. If you can catch that first fish you should be able to determine what the last few food sources were. Always keep an eye out for hatching insects. Matching the hatch is just as important on a stream as it is on the lake. Gravel on the stream bottom is the home for many nymphs, and a great place for fish to find dinner. Low light periods are the best time to spot fish in these places as they feel that they can't be easily seen. Strong hatches may also bring fish into feeding water during the day and occasion-ally they can be seen rising or tailing in very shallow water. Once again feeding water and holding water can be the same thing. In a wide open run of water, fish may have no need to leave. The water is slow enough for them to rest and plenty of food can be taken without exerting much energy. This moderate moving water is a excellent place to find the larger fish on a stream.

Oxygen plays an important role to fish in a stream. Warmer water can't dissolve as much oxygen as cooler water can. In warmer waters look for fish to be by incoming streams or just behind rapids where the water is aerated. Reading the water in a stream could also be called "common sense stream fishing." It's just as simple as know-ing where not to waste time casting. Techniques vary from each situation. There are a few basic ones that experienced anglers have modified into their own. Streamer fishing can be done in a variety of ways. Casting, letting the fly swing down the river is very effec-tive. I prefer to cast and retrieve the fly with long to short pulls. In the deeper water I prefer to use sinking line while a weighted pattern and a dry line can also do the trick. There are countless ways to fish

Dave Campbell drifting along

Casting in the mist - Photo by Gerry Frederick

streamers and they all have their moments.

Nymphing has gained a great deal of respect by anglers over the last few years. The art of matching the hatch has become very challenging and rewarding. High-stick nymphing is only one of a handful of techniques. Indicators have allowed us to set our flies at the proper depth and watch for a strike. Some rivers do not allow this practice and you should always check the regulations before using it. When you are fishing with indicators a tight line must be kept. Free drifts and keeping the nymph as close to the bottom as possible will increase your success. Covering the water with a variety of nymphing methods can turn a slow day of fishing around.

Dry fly fishing is arguably the best form of angling around. Anything from a gentle sip to an angry gulp sends my heart racing. Fishing the dry fly is generally easier than fishing streamers or dries. Most trout key in on certain hatches throughout the day and in some cases it's possible to dry fly fish for days at a time. Patterns like the Bullet Head Hopper or Simulator can work even when the naturales are not available. It's important to free drift your fly in most cases. There are a few exceptions like when you want to hop a hopper across the water or skitter a caddis along a clam slick. Keeping a tight line is a must, there's nothing worse than seeing your fly go under and setting the hook only to find you had too much slack line. Casting downstream, upstream and across can all be effective. I've found that proper presentation is just as important as choosing the right fly.

Successful Lake Fishing

Venturing out to a new lake can be a real challenge. I find myself looking around and not really knowing where to start. I think we all can feel this way when looking at unfamiliar water. There's something about fishing new water that I enjoy. The tales of 20 pounders or an alpine lake with a fish a cast, I just feel a need to find out what it's really like myself. Before I even unload the boat I like to look around for possible fish holding places. If it's spring time I'll look for shoals full of weed, if it's summer I'll look for those cool drop-offs. Just as on the stream, turning over a log or some rocks can prove rewarding. A freshly emerged damsel draws a smile over any experienced anglers face.

Once on the water look for any sign of a hatch. This takes some guess work as you won't really know what the fish are taking until you feel that hard pull on the end of your line. Searching patterns are very important at this time. Most anglers have their "ace in the hole." I tend to put a lot of faith in the Marabou Leech while others like Halfbacks or scuds. That first fish is very important. Using a stomach pump can show you the last few items taken by the fish. After looking at what the fish have eaten you should try to match it as closely as possible.

The lake itself can be divided up into four separate zones. The shoreline zone is where fish spawn and generally little feeding is done here. The shoal is where the majority of the feeding takes place throughout the year. The water is warmer here in the spring and fall and insects are abundant. Chironomids to leeches will all be found and fish are very aware of this. Summer can push the fish into the deeper, cooler water, but as the shoal cools down in the evening fish will move up once again to feed into the night. The drop-off zone is important as well. Many insects live deeper and make their move to the shoreline before they hatch. Dragonflies for example, swim or crawl to the shoreline just once in their life time. During this emergence swim they may be taken by fish from the deep water zone to the shoreline. Fish spend much of their summer day time on the drop-off. It's cool enough and has plenty of feed. The deep water zone is often where the big fish hold. Trollers have an advantage and in some lakes it's necessary to get down over 100 feet. Fish cool themselves here in the summer and the fly fisher has difficulty reaching them. Many lakes only reach a maximum depth of about

50 feet. This is a good depth because the bottom can still hold enough feed and the fly fisher can reach the bottom with most available sinking lines.

There are countless methods of fly fishing on lakes. The common day fly fisher most likely has at least a couple rods and a few lines. When people ask how to fly fish, I like to start people off on the right foot. Trolling in a float tube is easy and at times it's extremely effective. For a beginner fly fisher it's very important to get the feel of fighting a fish on the reel and off the reel. Float tubing brings almost every aspect of fly fishing together. When deciding what lines to use it's simply a matter of imitating the natural movements of the insect your imitating. For instance, it makes sense to fish a mayfly dun on the surface with dry line. Rods and reels are for the most part, just personal preference. Three lines I consider necessary include a dry line and two sinking lines, a fast sink and a slow sink. If you are a beginner, I think it's best to try and get out with someone more experienced. Most quality anglers have all learned from someone older and better, no amount of reading or watching can compete with hands on learning.

Angling Etiquette

With the gaining popularity of our sport today and the increase in traffic, it's important for us as anglers to not only respect the environment but each other as well. Too many times I have been anchored on a shoal, catching trout, and finding my line being almost cut off by a trolling motor. While I'm sure that this has happened to most of us at one time or another, it happens all too often today.

Lakes

We all need to be a little more careful when fishing in crowed waters. I float tube often and while float tubes are great, remember that your moving backwards and vision is limited. With many of our lakes being so clear, fish are easily "spooked" by any sudden movements. Noises such as a loud anchor being dropped or a gas engine running can slow down the fishing completely. It's a good idea to stay at least 300 feet from the closest boat. Many inexperienced anglers think that if someone is catching fish then that must be where the fish are. Of course if you have spent much time on the water you will know this is not true. Avoiding conversation is also appreciated by most. When I go fishing I like to enjoy the silence, someone asking every question makes me want to pack up and leave. In most cases I've spent a good deal of time trying to figure out what's working, it's not often that I would just pass along that information. On one last note, should a problem arise it's always better to walk away or just keep quiet. Sometimes people just don't know what their doing. A kind comment would at least give the fellow angler a better understanding of angling etiquette.

On the stream, a few rules of etiquette change. Fish and anglers are often condensed into smaller areas and fish tend to hold in very specific areas. On many of our rivers walking at least an hour to a good hole is the norm. Getting there only to have a drift boat beat you by a few feet and then fish the water is incredibly frustrating. Most experienced guides or anglers would and should have the courtesy to lift up the rods and carefully drift through. After all, they have the ability to cover much more water in a day than someone on foot. Walk and wade anglers always have the right of way. I think that boats should stay at least 200 yards away and pass by on the opposite side of the river. The same goes for anyone stopping for a break. It's best that the anglers pass on and respect that person's water. This goes for both shore anglers and drifters. When other anglers are encountered on the water stay as far away as possible. Crossing the river upstream can cause silting down stream. In general it's best to stay at least 500 feet away. One should also remember that most remote areas of our streams are not cared for by anyone other than the user. Garbage should always be removed and fire pits cleaned up. Overall if we give fellow anglers their space and deserved respect, we will all enjoy the water together.

Anglers on shore should have rights to the pool they're fishing

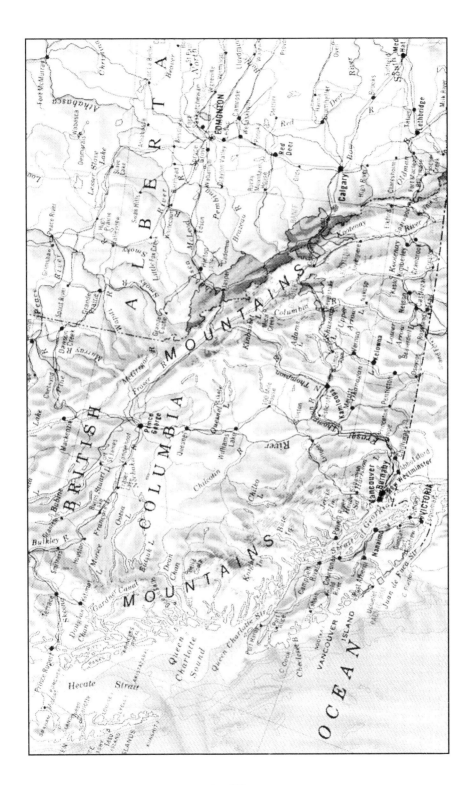

British Columbia's Region 1

With waters like the Campbell, Nimpkish and the Cowichan, the Vancouver Island region has been known as a fly fishers paradise for over a hundred years in B.C. Roderick Haig-Brown knew the Campbell River as his home water. For many years he fished and wrote of the waters in region 1 and many anglers have him to thank for his sharing of great knowledge. A region like this is uncommon due to its variety of game fish. Although it may be well known for the fantastic steelhead and salmon fishing offered, trout and bass can be found as well. Many lesser well known rivers still do not see much attention and angling can be superb.

Lakes can get over looked on the island but there are a few good ones. Alice Lake and Victoria Lake hold some good sized rainbows and cutties. Both lakes have boat launches and fishing can be good all year round. If you enjoy hiking into lakes for good rainbow fishing, The Forbidden Plateau Lakes about 25 km west of Courtenay offer some of the best if you hit it right. Be sure to read Barry Alldred's article on the Cowichan for a good view of what fishing can be like on many of the islands rivers.

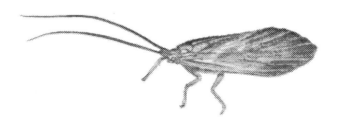

Barry Alldred

Born and raised in the Cowichan Valley has given Barry Alldred many great angling opportunities. Barry lived in Lake Cowichan for 20 years before moving to Duncan. He has had the pleasure of fishing the Cowichan River for almost 40 years and knows it as good as anyone. Barry is the owner of Squaretail Guide Service and runs a 16' fiberglass drift boat. Barry supplies all equipment needed for experiencing the trip of a life time. Specializing in fly fishing steelhead on the lower river has allowed Barry to help clients understand his home water and get into some hard fighting trophy fish that the lower Cowichan is famous for. Barry Alldred can be reached at (250) 748-3929.

The Cowichan River
Barry Alldred

The Cowichan River, a small river by comparison to many of B.C. rivers, flows into the Strait of Georgia at Cowichan Bay, near the City of Duncan. Duncan is located on the south east coast of Vancouver Island, about 40 min. north of Victoria on the Island Highway. About 50 km's long as a fish swims, the Cowichan River drains out of Cowichan Lake at the town of Lake Cowichan.

Cowichan Lake is one of the largest lakes on Vancouver Island at almost 33 km's long and 2 km's wide at its widest point. Cowichan Lake probably best known for its Coastal cutthroat which run to 7 - 8 lbs. The lake also contains rainbow, Dolly Varden and kokanee. Cowichan Lake sits at the head of the Cowichan Valley, a wide fairly flat valley bottom bordered to the north and south by two low rolling mountain ranges. Lake Cowichan in the heart of the valley, a town built by logging and sawmills, is known as "The Gateway to the West Coast".

The Cowichan River contains 3 species of salmon and 4 species of trout. The spring salmon (chinook, king) enter the river in August and run through till October. Their size runs from 5 lbs to 30 lbs, with the average being about 10 - 15 lbs. Spring salmon spend anywhere from 2-5 years in the ocean before returning to spawn. The Cowichan has a run of Jack Springs which are male Springs that have only spent one year in the ocean before returning to spawn. When fishing Spring salmon in the river, a spring under 50 cm in length is classified as a Jack Spring. The coho salmon (Silvers) start returning around the end of September and run into December, the peak being around the end of October. The Cowichan was once world famous for its Big Northerns, coho running into the high teens. But these fish are now few and far between. The average size is now 4 - 6 lbs. Coho can be quite responsive to flies and on the right day can provide a lot of action on the fly rod. Low returns the last couple of years has forced the DFO to put catch and release regulations on the river for coho. Anyone planning a trip to the Cowichan for coho should phone ahead for information first.

Chum salmon run between the middle of October and the middle of December. Classified as a commercial salmon, chums are no retention in fresh water. Not a pretty fish because they enter the river in full spawning color. They are gaining popularity as a catch and release fishery because of their size, 10 lbs on average, with many fish well into the high teens. They are very aggressive and will hit almost anything you put in the water (and run back to the ocean with it). While gaining popularity with some they remain a nuisance to others, because their heavy numbers make it hard to angle for early run steelhead.

Christmas is the traditional start to the steelhead season, although the steelhead actually start coming into the river around the end of November beginning of December. It's not until Christmas that the first main runs of steelhead start to show up. Steelhead enter the river until the beginning of April, with March being the peak month. The early fish tend to be larger fish averaging 8 lbs, with many fish in the teens and the odd trophy going better than 20 lbs. The March runs tend to have more fish but the average size drops to about 6 lbs.

The Cowichan River, ranked among the best rivers in British Columbia is one of the top 3 steelhead rivers on Vancouver Island. The Stamp/Somass system and Gold River are generally accepted as the other two. The Cowichan has been having some problems lately, over the past few years bank erosion has become a major concern. Floods have opened up several clay seams which can color the water leaving the river unfishable for several weeks after a heavy rain. Fishermen planning a winter steelhead trip to the Cowichan should phone ahead for river conditions.

The Cowichan River is divided in half by Skutz Falls. Skutz Falls is considered class 5 - 6 rapids depending on water height. To allow fish passage to the upper river there is a series of 3 fish ladders. Although all species of trout and salmon are found throughout the river, trout fishing is done primarily above the falls. To explain trout fishing on the Cowichan would take a couple hours of serious studying. Start by checking out the fishing synopsis. Once glance will show you the Cowichan is the most regulated river in British Columbia! Bar none. The saying, "You need to be a Philadelphia lawyer to understand the regs!" was cloned on the Cowichan. Now let's see if I can make these regulations a little easier to understand. Let me take you on a quick drift down the top end of the Cowichan, where most of the regulations are in effect. So holding this book in your left hand and the fishing synopsis in your right, join me in my drift boat as I head down river from Cowichan Lake describing fishing boundaries as I come to them.

There is a weir across the mouth of the lake, this is the start of the river, and upstream boundary for fish retention. Always watch for gear and bait restrictions and seasonal closures. About 2 km's down stream you pass under the second old steel railway bridge. This is the trestle at Greendale Road and the downstream boundary for fish retention. About 4-5 hundred yards downstream from the trestle entering from the left, is Stanley Creek, a small rather hard to spot fishing boundary sign, mounted in a tree on the opposite side of the river. Stanley Creek is the downstream boundary of seasonal closures and the upstream boundary of the fly fishing only section. There is a regulation allowing the retention of hatchery trout/char from Stanley Creek to the mile 70.2 bridge. There are no hatchery stocks released above Skutz Falls, the river above the falls is managed as wild stocks only and this regulation is only for the odd hatchery steelhead or trout that wanders up past the falls.

The fly fishing only section takes up about the next 5 km's of river, until you pass under the mile 70.2 bridge. An old wooden railway bridge no longer being used. Both the CPR and the CNR, the two railroads that used to service the Cowichan Valley, have been taken out of service. Then from the mile 70.2 bridge to Skutz Falls, the river has gear and bait restrictions. Skutz Falls is a natural boundary dividing the river into two sections, the upper and lower river. From the falls to the estuary the river has gear, bait and retention restrictions. (Once again, check the current synopsis)

There is a lot or private land along the Cowichan River. You should check with the local tackle shops (Bucky's Sport Shop Ltd or Outdoor Explorers) in Duncan. (H & H Guns and Sporting Supplies) in Lake Cowichan. Glenora, a rural farm area south west of Duncan, is home to the Duncan Fish and Game Association Rifle Range. The parking lot is the start of the Fish and Game Club's Hiking Trail which runs along the south shore of the river. The trail is 19.5 km long from the Fish and Game Club to Skutz Falls. The trail travels through natural forest lands backing away from the river with many side trails branching off down to the river. At Skutz Falls another trail starts at the Provincial Park and runs up the north side of the upper river for about 8-10 km's before running into private land.

Upper river boat launch is best at the weir and road pool on

Greendale Road. Take out only at Skutz Falls (a dangerous take out right at the crest of the falls). Please make sure you know exactly where it is. On the lower river you may launch at Stoltz Provincial Park, Sandy Pool Park and Heritage Road. Take out only under the Silver Bridge in Duncan. A rough take out up a riprap bank and unfortunately there is no trailer access. Always check ahead for river conditions when floating the Cowichan. Unstable banks cause sweepers and log jams, making it dangerous for inexperienced boaters.

The three major insect species in the Cowichan are stone flies, caddis and mayflies. The stone flies in winter are black and brown and about size 10, in spring are golden stones about size 6. The caddis works well throughout the spring in size 12 and 14. I prefer a Elk Hair Caddis in brown or gold. A Gold Rib Hare's Ear is a good searching pattern throughout the year when nymphing. Mayflies also are found throughout the spring. A mayfly Pheasant Tail nymph in size 12-16 works excellent and a March Brown or Blue Dun in size 12-16 will imitate adults. There are several other hatches found depending on the season. Be prepared to fish terrestrials if the opportunity presents itself.

The Cowichan is known around the world for its brown trout. Stocked in the early 1900's, the Cowichan now has a very healthy population. These fish average 16"-18" with good number of fish larger and a few real trophies in the 25" to 30" range. These stocks are not healthy for no reason, these fish while being very aggressive feeders, are very wary. The browns tend to be a challenge for even the most experienced anglers.

Browns are found throughout the river. Here lies a slight controversy as to whether or not there are two strains of browns in the Cowichan. In the lower river, only below Skutz Falls, you'll find a strain of browns very silver in coloration and white bellied. None of the typical coloring of the German brown except a slight yellowish color to the fins. The Locklevian brown or sea trout as they are called in Scotland, are a sea run brown trout. Possibly one explanation could be that some of the eggs brought over from Europe in the early 1900's could have been mixed strains of both German and Scottish browns. The lower river has German browns as well. These fish have dropped down from the upper river naturally stocking the lower river and have also been hatchery stocked from brood stock taken from the upper river. There are no hatchery fish of any species released above the falls, keeping the upper river as wild stocks only.

Rainbow trout are primarily found in the upper river. There are 3 different types of rainbow in the Cowichan. The 1st are the resident fish residing year around in the river. These fish average 8"-13" in length with a few up to 18". The second are lake fish which drop down out of the lake during the winter to spawn. These fish average 12"-16" and run over 20". They drop down from the lake in early winter and spend the winter in the upper reaches of the river to spawn. With the dropping water levels in the spring and the spring closure of the weir, they migrate back up into the lake. The 3rd type of rainbow are in fact steelhead smolts. These small trout, averaging 10" are often mistaken as resident fish. With the drastically declining steelhead stocks, over fishing these smolts, especially on the lower river where the majority of the rainbows are steelhead smolts, is a major concern.

The Cowichan also holds a small population of resident cut-throat. Found mostly in the upper reaches of the river, these fish average 8"-12" with some up around 16"-18". A once healthy run of sea run cutthroat on the lower river, averaging 14"-15" with

Searun Brown on the Lower Cowichan

some over 20", is now protected by a year around catch and re-lease regulation. These fish are worth the time spent, one of the prettiest sea run cuts you'll find, they are very strong fighters.

The Cowichan River is very special in that it is one of the only rivers in B.C. that can be fished all year round. By prac-ticing catch and release we can insure many more enjoyable angling seasons to come.

British Columbia's Region 2

Even as the most populated region in British Columbia, region 2 has incredible angling opportunities. Blessed with great rivers such as the Coquihalla, Harrison, Skagit and the Vedder, anglers flock from around the world to fish these great waters. Countless rivers and countless fishing locations, one has the chance to get away from the crowds or join them. Similarly to region 1, region 2 is best known for steelhead and salmon fishing. Fishing can be great throughout the year on most streams.

Runs of steelhead and salmon have sunken to all time lows on some rivers so anglers should not expect the fishing to be as good as it was years ago. There are many reasons for the downfall in fish numbers and no single reason can be completely blamed. One thing is for sure, we all need to protect this valuable resource. The large lakes of the lower mainland are not known as friendly towards fly fishers. Trolling will often produce the better fish in lakes like Alouette and Pitt although there are some fly fishing opportunities. Many small lakes can be found and the ones you drive to can get a little crowded. If your serious about small lake fly fishing, look for some more remote hike-in lakes. A small group of lakes near Chilliwack Lake can be excellent for rainbows. Lindeman and Greendrop have plenty of good size trout and Flora can produce the odd lunker. Float tubes are a big advantage on these lakes. Whether fishing the Vedder or one of the lakes in region 2, be prepared for some company. If you are willing to put up with the crowds, the fishing can be great.

Guide's Choices for the Lower Mainland

Chehalis River

Much of this 20 km long river is guarded in a canyon and therefore difficult to access in some places. A good run of hatchery enhanced steelhead in the winter and a fair run of them in the summer months. Coho fishing in the late fall is excellent. Many fly fishers have trouble in the canyon, but the lower stretches offer the fly fisher some great opportunities. Crowds can become a problem when the fishing is good, but on the other hand they sure let you know if the fish are there. Standard steelhead and salmon patterns will suffice.

Vedder River

Arguably the best river in the valley and definitely the busiest. Winter steelheading is very popular and most anglers concentrate on them. As with most rivers in the valley, coho fishing is also popular. Just as the coho fishing slows down, the steelhead start to run. December to April is the best time to try and hook into one of these world famous steelhead.

Pitt River

The area surrounding the Pitt River and lake stands out as one of the last wilderness retreats in the lower mainland. Pitt Lake is over 20 kms long and fly fishing is generally poor. The lake tends to become windy very fast and it's dangerous for small boats. The river on the other hand has some excellent fly fishing. The Upper Pitt contains steelhead from Feb-April, coho from Oct-Dec and large rainbows, cutthroat and Dollies are found in the Pitt all year. A very scenic river that should not be missed.

Squamish River

A large river with an excellent reputation that it has had trouble keeping up with in the last few years. So many fishers in region 2 make it almost impossible to angle anywhere in solitude. Late winter steelhead run from about mid March til late April and the fishing can be great as long as the river stays clean. Dollies once were easy to catch but overfishing has caused them to become a rarity. The layout and beauty of the Squamish makes it the perfect river to fly fish, and that is precisely why people return every season.

Gerry Frederick

Gerry Frederick is a veteran fly fisher who has fly fished all over North America for more than 27 years. He has operated a fly fishing school and guide service for the last two years, where he shares his years of hard earned experience with beginners and other veterans alike. Gerry's fly fishing school "Rocky Mountain Angler" is noted for it's high quality fly fishing and fly tying classes. Both on and off the water Gerry can turn anyone into a more productive angler. Gerry also writes a weekly fly fishing column for several newspapers in the Canadian Rockies. Gerry can be reached at 250-489-4053.

Where To Start Fly Fishing When Away From Home

Gerry Frederick

Sometimes "Angling in the shadow of the Rockies" can be a little overwhelming. So many waters to pick from and so little time. From New Mexico to British Columbia, the Rockies provide the best trout fishing in North America. I don't believe many fisherman will argue with this assessment. Here in lies the dilemma. Where to start. I suggest we start at home.

As is true with all outdoor activities preparation is important. Every fisherman has a few stories to tell of fouled trips from lack of preparation. I truly believe that I hold the crown. I'm also sure the other members of the royal court come from my family. Perhaps more than anyone I can address the tragedy of poor preparation. My trouble is I'm a fly fishing nut. I get excited anticipating each trip. This excitement causes me to sometimes forget a few very important items: fly boxes, oars, fly rod, fly reels, and on and on. What I'm trying to say is, it's very easy to leave home unprepared.

Check Your Gear

Take time to check all the gear you plan to utilize on your fishing trip. It doesn't take long to check for worn out components, missing reel screws and the like. Clean and inspect very closely all the fly lines you'll bring. Don't forget to make an inventory of the fishing vest. In keeping with historical fly fishing tradition bring four of five time more stuff than you'll ever use. This small detail helps build confidence and gives the outward appearance of someone who know his or her way around the fishing hole.

If you have chosen a fishing destination that is at all remote bring some extra gear. This may include everything from underwear to complete rod and reel set ups. Extra equipment will set your mind at ease and help keep you focused on the fishing. Remember if a little is good, a lot must be better.

Pick Your Angling Destination

Location is everything. The fly fishing opportunities in the Rockies are endless. Maps, magazine articles, books and fish stories all play big factors when we are searching out new waters to fish.

In the south east region of British Columbia where I call home, I generally know what to expect. I start with location. I have fly fished this region for more than ten years, guided for two years. Once I decide where to fish I can draw on some of my own history. From time to time I have the good fortune to take my fly fishing obsession on the road. I always pick new water to fish. Topographic maps make this process a lot faster. The most recent updated maps if you can find them. I like to pick 3 or 4 locations in a given region. When one doesn't work out I can move on.

When traveling on fishing trips in the Rockies it's important to get as much local input as possible. The local fly fishing information we gather can help with what we can expect. Most local fly shops and tackle dealers will give us, "out-of-towners", the straight goods on hot spots and what to start with. They all have an interest in fisherman doing well in their backyard.

Trip Planning

It can't be understated, the importance of trip planning. A lot of time can be wasted if a river is closed or out of season after we have traveled three or four hours to get there. Get the info anyway you can. Time permitting, write for as much information as you can get your hands on. Sometimes the library can get us off on the right foot. I believe the map is still number one. Without a good map fishing trips away from familiar surroundings rarely go well. A popular trick in my family is to keep a good collection of topographical maps in the "John" along with all the fly fishing magazines. Another point to remember is where you plan to stay. I strongly suggest a reservation at a camp ground or motel. In 1994 I went on a fly fishing trip to the Bitteroot region of Montana for five days. I started looking for a motel at 9:30 at night and at midnight found myself parked in the car at the water edge tilting the seat back for a few hours sleep. Even for a fishing nut like myself, sleeping in the car was not what I had in mind.

There was one small positive however. When I opened my eyes I was looking over the Bitteroot River and a dozen or so fish feeding near the bank. I was rigged and casting for them in a record 8 or 10 minutes.

K.I.S.S.

A very large part of my fly fishing philosophy is Keep It Simple Stupid, K.I.S.S. The simple approach works well when fishing unfamiliar waters. Keeping the gear and flies down to a simple, manageable assortment. This not only helps with traveling, but helps keep us focused on the task at hand. Fishing a new region will keep us busy enough. Go with what you know. Utilize the flies and techniques that work at home.

Most fly fishers, experienced and beginners alike, don't need me to tell them to keep it simple. Sometimes we can get caught up with new gear and techniques. Learning and using new techniques is important to any advancement in individual success. I believe it's important to try new things. That can be one of the best aspects of fly fishing. However, when I suggest, go with what you know, I mean just that. Take a fly and a technique that you have the most success with and utilize it. This will keep you in your comfort zone. After all the important pre-trip preparation is done, we're ready. Ready for challenging new adventure away from home. When fishing in unfamiliar areas, maps are important as are local angling regulations. Fly fishing new waters presents an array of challenges. Most are welcome unknowns that fly fishing nuts like myself look forward to conquering. A large part of the appeal is showing off your ability to read water and catch fish. Most of the time you're only showing off to yourself.

Getting Started

After you have arrived at the waters edge, be it lake or stream, slow down a little. Now it's important to stop and observe everything you can. Make a mental check list. My list is pretty simple; air temperature, clouds, sun, wind, water level. But most important of all, what bugs do I see. On the water, in the water or flying around. Look into the bushes and trees near the water edge. Even give them a shake to see what falls or flies out. For example, if you shake out a caddis from a nearby bush, take note of the size and color.

Sometimes we get lucky and it's clear from the start what is available to trout at the spot we've picked. Most of the time it's not. That's O.K., now we have to go with what we know. Keep with the K.I.S.S. method and don't over think it. The more experienced fly fishers will have one or more "go to" setups that work for them. Beginners need to fall back on the fundamentals.

My most common suggestion is stay below the surface as long as you can hold out. Find a spot on the stream or lake that looks fishy. In rivers start down stream, behind a rock that looks like it may hold fish. Close to a river bank if it's deep enough is another spot to try. Tie on your favorite nymph (I like a Beadhead Pheasant Tail) on a long leader, ten feet or so. Floating line works best in water less than six feet deep.

Make sure you fish an area thoroughly. Cast several times in and around the chosen spot. Adjust the speed of the retrieve every other cast. Watch the line very closely for any movement caused by a fish. Watch for fish following the fly. Don't change the fly, move to a new spot and try it all again. Be sure you have fished the first few spots thoroughly before changing flies.

I have often said that the presentation is more important than fly selection. Be sure you have done all you can with the fly and location before changing. Go with what you know or what you have learned. All too often anglers use the fly as the excuse for no fish when actually it's presentation or location. If you pick a productive fly and fish an area completely, than it could be said the fish are not there or just not interested. Another reason the fish won't take could be you stumbled up to the fishing hole and just spooked them. If that's a possibility just move on and come back later. It has been my experience that fish usually are not as picky as we have been lead to believe.

The Flies

The flies you choose are up to you. If you have experience fly fishing in the Rockies you may already have a comprehensive fly selection to start with. Every experienced fly fisher of course has his or her favorite fly patterns. These are usually flies that they have a good history with and have learned how to fish. Have confidence in the flies you choose. Don't add too many unfamiliar flies to your box too quickly. Learn what each fly imitates and how to fish it; what depth and speed it should have in the water.

The Pheasant Tail Nymph and other popular common nymphs like stone's and caddis nymphs catch trout all the time. Trust them, they work all over the world. In the waters of the Rocky Mountains these flies and a few more old standbys will catch fish if the fish are there and the fly is presented the way they want it.

Here are my fly suggestions. I feel these few flies in a variety of colors and sizes make up a great selection. Six flies in four sizes made up in three colors offer the fly fisher 72 flies, a good place to start.

- Pheasant Tail (with or without Beadhead) sizes 10 - 18

- Hares Ear (with or without Beadhead) sizes 10 - 18

- Beadhead Prince - sizes 8 - 16

- Heavy Stone (Black, tan, olive, yellow) sizes 4 - 10

- Latex Caddis (Tan, olive, rusty brown) sizes 8 -14

- Chironomid (Black, green, brown, red) sizes 10 - 18

Remember keep it simple. Make it easy on yourself and easy on the fish. Trout, certainly Rocky Mountain trout, are not as picky as you may think. All trout are opportunistic feeders. They will feed on what ever looks and acts like food. Sure enough they have their picky periods. That's when we need to get serious. Stay with the fundamentals and fish the flies in the box properly. Look forward to those challenging days. Beginners will have more than their share of picky fish. Conquering tough days on the water is very rewarding. More so when fishing away from home. A good days fly fishing in new waters, perhaps using a different technique or fly only adds to the life experience. Fishing abilities can only grow with experience.

Other chapters in this book will help with more details and suggestions. Fly fishing offers a large array of methods and gear. After a food fundamental start it is fun to try something new. Once the fly fisher has a good understanding of nymph fishing the natural progression is to dry fly. Top water is fun, some fly fishers believe it's the only way to go. The truth is it's not always the most productive.

It is widely believed that trout feed under the surface 80% or more of the time. That's why nymphs are a good place to start. They are also a lot easier to fish and learn. Trout are a little more willing and less selective under the surface. Cutthroat trout are the most gullible of all, and the Rockies are full of them. If you're lucky enough to fly fish the Rockies you'll learn quickly what works. Get prepared, steal all the hot information you can and remember to K.I.S.S. Keep It Simple Stupid. You'll have a great time and whatever your level of experience you'll learn something.

The Interior Lakes of British Columbia

Gordon Honey is the premier guide in the Kamloops area of British Columbia. Gordon has the skills and knowledge that are required when fishing these lakes. In the next few pages he will share with us some of the knowledge he has gained over his many years of fly fishing. As these lakes in region 3 and 8 are so different than others in the province, it's important to have a good understanding of what to expect before attempting battle with the great Kamloops rainbows.

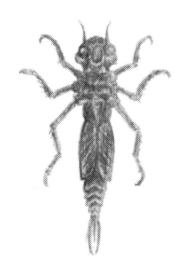

Gordon Honey

Let me introduce myself. Prior to my current professional piscatorial pursuit, I spent 27 years in the television broadcast industry, which concluded in 1992. Following much soul searching (about 30 seconds worth), and with a little jingle in my pocket, I decided to turn this opportunity and my passion for fly fishing, into a career. To date I have chased Kamloops trout with a fly rod for 39 years, the last 5 as a professional guide.

I dabble at writing, a weekly column "Of Feathers & Fins" for the "Kamloops Daily News" and under the same byline for a major outdoor web site "The BC Adventure Network" and Sea to Sky's Publications "The Interiors Outdoor Adventure Journal". I still play at television with a Micro series "Of Feathers & Fins" a 10 episodes series on stillwater tactics. I am partners with and produce Brian Chan's instructional video series "Fly fishing Strategies for Stillwaters". I'm also on the Pro-Staff for Lamiglas.

I do not and will not purport to be an expert. I have only known two fly fishers I would call experts, Jack Shaw and the late Heber Smith, pioneers in fly fishing for Kamloops trout. Being humbled on more than one occasion I think I have learned a little and have been blessed by a circle of quality fly-fisher pals who have taught me more than I could ever teach them.

The High Desert Lakes of British Columbia
Gordon Honey

The quality stillwaters region of British Columbia defined geographically as, south of Prince George in the north, east of the Coastal mountain range to the west, and east to the foothills of the Rocky Mountains. The southern area extends to the U.S./Canadian border. This is the central interior, a diverse land of alpine meadows, rolling ranch land and semiarid desert valleys.

The number and diversity of the lakes within this region is astounding, for example in the Kamloops region alone, there is two hundred lakes within a 60 mile radius of the city. The central interior of British Columbia is truly the stillwater capital of the world, a fly fisher's paradise!

The Quarry

The premier sport fish of the region is the Kamloops trout Salmo kamloops, named in 1892 by Dr. D. S. Jordan of Stanford University. The Kamloops trout is a sub species of the rainbow trout Salmo gairdneri now referred to by biologists as Salmo gairdneri kamloops. It is a common belief that the Kamloops trout evolved from the Thompson River Steelhead, resulting in their bright silver coloring and their world renown fighting qualities! Kamloops trout are now available to anglers the world over, thanks to stocking exchange programs, can be found as far away as New Zealand, and are currently stocked in lakes in Oregon and California.

Kamloops trout range in size from one half pound to as much twenty pounds (Interior anglers generally size fish by pounds rather than inches). These sizes vary from lake to lake based on the following factors: lake depth, water chemistry and average temperature, shoal structure, aquatic vegetation, and impacting on all of these factors, elevation. Larger fish are more common in lakes at elevations of 1000 ft, to a maximum of 5000 ft. Mountain lakes beyond the 5000 ft. level do not support significant numbers of large fish, due to water chemistry and a limited growth period created by winter ice, and the shorter spring and summer seasons. These lakes are populated by an abundance of smaller fish, and provide a wonderful dry fly experience. Large fish lakes are typically shallow, averaging approximately fifteen feet to a maximum of twenty to twenty-five feet, full of nutrients and aquatic vegetation, these lakes are almost one vast shoal! The single major factor responsible for this productive fishery is the rainshadow effect created by the Coastal and Cascade Mountain Ranges, resulting in annual rain fall less than 9 inches and therefore a high desert. Respected American writer Ted Leesen captured the essence of our lakes and fish in his June 1997 article in FIELD & STREAM. "Rainshadow Rainbows" he wrote "By any measure, the lakes of southern British Columbia must be reckoned the crown jewels of the rainshadow waters. The city of Kamloops is the angling epicenter, and the Kamloops trout is the heart of the game. A girthy, muscular fish, with the luster of machined titanium that hints of its genetic roots in the Thompson River strain of steelhead." He continued "I can think of worse ways to spend a lifetime than fishing the lodgepole-rimmed waters where all the trout have wings"

Our Ministry Of Environment, Fisheries Branch has been very successful with the genetic engineering of Triploid females. These sterile females grow slower, bigger and live longer, there are now 30 lakes with Triploid rainbows and some Eastern brook trout. Additional species that are of interest to the stillwater fly fisher in B.C.'s Central Interior, would be Kokanee O.nerka kennerlyi, a fresh water sockeye salmon that has residualized and remains in fresh water. Kokanee have become a respected sport fish and are generally found in our larger bodies of water. A large kokanee would be three pounds, while the average would be one pound (patterns, tactics, and key time periods parallel those of the Kamloops trout).

Considered by the majority to be inferior in sport quality, the third and final stillwater species available to the fly angler, is the Eastern Brook trout Salvelinus fontinalis, introduced years ago in an attempt to reduce the pressure on our better Kamloops trout lakes during the winter ice fishing. The brookie does not receive much angling pressure during ice off, and can therefore provide an interesting and challenging alternative, especially during the heat of summer. Tactics, patterns and habitat can be very different from that of the Kamloops trout, providing a pleasant diversion; average sizes are comparative to the Kokanee.

The Season

Historical averages indicate May 1 as typical ice off and beginning of the season. But dependent on the severity of the winter and the elevation, many valley lakes are free of ice as early as late March and early April. A word of caution however; check the Fresh Water Angling Regulation's carefully before venturing out, as many lakes are closed and do not open for angling until May 1. It is usually only the very keen and the very hardy who venture out in March and early April. Although many days can be bright and warm, dress in layers and be prepared for sudden squalls bringing chilly winds. Wind, our friend when it assists in the vital oxygenation of the lakes, or when it provides us the gentle cover of a fly fisher's riffle when casting in shallower water, but oh how we curse it, when the anchors no longer hold, and we are blown off the lake! The season moves into full swing as May begins, the only negative you may experience at this time might be, arriving at the chosen water, finding it slightly off clarity or murky, the lake has turned over or mixed as all lakes must do in the spring and fall to remain properly oxygenated. When a lake has turned over the poor water quality impacts on the angling as well, this condition typically lasts for two weeks. As the days warm and become longer the insect hatches increase as the water warms, stillwater fly fishing has begun in earnest.

In June, and as July approaches the warm weather of the Central Interior begins in earnest, valley temperatures in the Kamloops area, can reach upwards of 100°F. The fly fisher must now move to higher elevations, as the trout in valley lakes seek the cooler waters of the thermocline, feeding in the shallower waters of the shoals, only as the evenings approach. These conditions remain until the latter part of August when evening air temperatures begin to cool, as do the water temperatures. September brings the first frosts that touch the leaves of not only the deciduous forest trees, but also the exposed tips of the lakes aquatic vegetation. As the frosts increase through September and October, the larger fish return to the shoals and shallower water, where they can, at times, forage voraciously, sensing the return of winter and it's cover of ice and snow.

Tackle, Key Time Periods and Food Sources

Fly fishing stillwaters is perhaps a new experience for you and will require some adjustments not only in your traditional techniques, but also in the gear you use. Of the lakes in the Central Interior of B.C. 99.9% are not conducive to wading. Fly fishing requires the use of either a float tube or a boat. Many of the better lakes are quite large, making the use of a float tube limited or dangerous, tubes are ideal for the numerous smaller lakes. The vast majority of area angling is from boats; they are available for rent from fish camps or resorts.

Angling from a boat could very well be foreign to you, here are some thoughts:

Your boat should carry at least one anchor, (preferably two), you have much better control of your fly line, and therefore your ability to impart the correct action, of your chosen fly pattern.

Use a gasoline motor only on large lakes, using the oars to row quietly as you approach the shoal or drop-off you are going to fish.

Loose carpeting covering the interior bottom of the boat will protect your valuable fly line, keeping it clean from sand and grit, and will also help to muffle boat noise's especially in an aluminum hull.

Keep the area at your feet uncluttered, it is very frustrating when the fly line tangles in your fly bag or whatever else it can find. You would not be a happy angler, when you finally hook Walter and as he rips coiled line from the bottom, in the first powerful run, and the last coil of line wraps itself around the clutter; —- ping, Walter, with your tippet in tow, swims peacefully away!!

Wear soft soled shoes so, that if you do step on your fly line, it will happen, no damage will occur. Soft soles also help in muffling sounds as you move about.

Boat and Float Tube Etiquette

As you approach the key area and find that others have preceded you, row or paddle slowly and quietly, maintain a distance of at least 150 to 200 ft., from those already anchored. This should be especially noted when in a tube, as your depth perception is distorted by your proximity to the surface. As you move into position, never, ever come between another angler and the shoreline. Release your anchors quietly, an anchor thrown or splashed loudly will scatter fish and draw the ire of those around you.

Equipment Selection

Appropriate rod and line sizes, rod lengths and line types may vary, dependent upon, techniques, weather conditions and water depth. It is not uncommon for an experienced, stillwater angler to carry four rods, completely setup for a day on the water. A much simpler method is to have two rods and reels set up, carrying various line types on spare spools.

Reels, need only a simple drag system, an exposed rim and the capacity to carry at least 100 yds. of backing.

Line types could be priorised as follows: floating; intermediate; full sink in rates of #1; #2; #3 and a #4 for August.

Selected rod and line weights, become personal preferences and may vary from 5 to 8 weights. If only one all round weight was to be decided upon, a 6 weight in two lengths, an 8° and a 9°ft. would be perfect. They can handle the larger fish, and can drive long casts into the wind when necessary.

Long casts, 60 to 80 ft., while not always essential, allow for more fishing time, as each retrieve is made. If you feel intimidated by this — don't be, practice before going on the water. A great deal of time can be spent sitting down when fly fishing from a boat, both for comfort, and at times to keep a low profile, it would therefore, be wise to practice casting from a sitting position as well.

Key Time Periods & Relative Food Sources

Immediately following ice off, prior to spring turn over, trout key on staple and constant food sources — leeches, fresh water shrimp (scuds) and chironomid (midges) larvae, commonly called bloodworms. May and early June is the primary chironomid period as trout gorge themselves on the pupae as they rise slowly to surface, in a vertical migration. This is an exciting time for the knowledgeable angler, fishing with floating lines and, dependent on the water depth, leaders of between 15 and 25 ft. in length are common. This type of angling requires long casts, and infinite patients as the retrieve must be slow, slow and slower still as the chironomids with no ability to swim, simply rise to surface as they writhe and twist. Your floating line becomes your strike indicator, so constant, hawk like attention, must be paid as even the smallest movement or twitch can be a take.

June and early July is a busy time for both Mother Nature and the fly fisher as various major hatches occur, sedges (caddis), mayflies (Callibaetis), damsel flies and dragonflies both the Darner (free swimmer) and the Gomphus (bottom walker) create the trout's menu! Being a keen observer is the key to success in any situation.

Late July and most of August become the most difficult, technical fly fishing of the entire season. Summer temperatures rise, and trout seek the cooler waters of the thermocline, fly fisher's must adapt in different ways, either maintaining the use of floating lines and dry fly's, while pursuing the smaller trout of the higher elevations, or patiently, probing the deeps with various sinking lines; for larger fish, imitating dragonflies, shrimp (scuds) and leech patterns. Changing to floating lines as the evening cools and the trout move to the shallows to forage on the shoals. It is not unusual, when under the cover of dusk then darkness, nocturnal sedge's (caddis); leviathan's named locally as Traveler's, perform their wild skating dance upon the serene moonlight water's; stimulating a feeding frenzy, accompanied by slashing rises; that live forever in the memory of anglers fortunate enough to experience, such an evening!

September and October are heralded by, flights of migrating water fowl, the crisp tonic of fall air, cool mornings, warm afternoons and active trout! This is the time of large fish as they prepare for the long winter months ahead. Frosts continue to thin the stand-up weeds of the shoals allowing room for the wide shoulders; nickel plated, slabs of fall to move and feed freely on the shoals. Life for the fly fisher becomes energized, as the trout's feeding preferences become simpler as they return to the staples once more. Bloodworms, leeches, dragons, scuds, water boatmen and some chironomid hatches combine to create a tremendous fishery.

As November approaches, and temperatures continue to fall, the increase of morning shore ice heralds the approach of winter. Life below the surface slows, light begins to fade, as curtain of ice is drawn relentlessly over the lake surface, our season of stillwater has ended.

British Columbia's Region 3

When I think of region 3, I think of lake fishing and trophy rainbows. With just the right mix of minerals and conditions, the lakes in this region become capable of holding tremendous insect life and subsequently tremendous rainbows. Centralized around Kamloops there is hundreds of lakes ranging in size from big to small with many of them holding the famed Kamloops rainbow. Anglers have come from all over to fish here and very few leave unsatisfied. Any fisher in B.C. owes thanks to the many techniques developed by fishers in region 3. Successful chironomid techniques came from here and countless famed anglers like Brian Chan and Jack Shaw have written of the glory and challenges of these beautiful lakes. Lakes like Lac Le Jeune, White, Roche, Peterhope and Knouff are just a few of the many beautiful fishing treasures. Countless small lakes are in this region and some feel that there are more quality waters here than in all the other regions combined.

Rivers can become overshadowed by the fame of the lakes. Sections of the Thompson have great rainbow fishing and the summer steelhead run should not be missed either. Rivers like the Adams and the Little can also be good. Whether you come to fish the lakes or streams the challenges and rewards will never be forgotten.

Neil Abbot

Neil Abbot was born in 1954 and raised in eastern Ontario where he spent his childhood and teenage years fishing the Rideau Valley. He moved to Vancouver in 1973 and began hiking, canoeing and fishing the more remote areas of B.C. After meeting his wife Georgi, they bought a travel trailer and float tubes and spent every weekend fly fishing.

They discovered the Logan Lake area in 1992 and seldom felt the need to fish elsewhere. In 1996 they left their Vancouver jobs and moved to Logan Lake where they now own and operate Logan Lake Fly Shop along with the Logan Lake Wine Shop. They spend every spare moment fishing the local lakes and enjoying the outdoors. Logan Lake fly shop can be reached at 250-523-9711.

Logan Lake Area Lakes
Neil Abbot

Framed by Kamloops Lake to the north, the Thompson River to the west, the Nicola River to the south and highway 5A to the east, lies British Columbia's finest small lake fly fishing for rainbow trout. Situated in the center of this area is the town site of Logan Lake. Within one hours drive, over 50 quality trout lakes covering an elevation of 2,000 - 5,000 feet above sea level can be accessed. Kamloops trout, once thought to be a separate species, are distinctive only by their environment. The waters of the area are extremely nutrient rich especially in calcium and the gentle rolling landscape results in lakes having relatively large shoal areas. These shoal areas produce the vegetation that provides habitat and food for the aquatic invertebrate. Kamloops trout will rarely graduate to food sources (minnows, amphibians) other than insects. Aquatic life is so abundant that little effort is required by trout to chase down prey. Under these conditions trout may put on weight at a rate of a pound or more per year. When hooked the Kamloops trout almost immediately break for the surface, tail walking and head shaking. Capable of larger runs, anglers are advised to have adequate backing spooled on their fly reels.

Larger trout over 5 lbs are regularly hooked but often lost, usually on the first jump. No where else will you see so many trout in the air. These fish love to jump. Although it is accepted a jumping fish is not feeding, it does show that they are active and more inclined to feed. Also a fly fisher can determine the position of trout in a lake by observing where trout are showing. Insect activity is of course climate induced and elevation is a variable that keen fly fishers can use to their advantage. Spring comes later and fall earlier at higher elevations. Lets say you missed the intense sedge hatches by a week or ten days at a 3,500 ft lake, chances are good that the sedges are just coming on at a 5,000 ft lake, of course this is determined by timing and intensity of hatches. On a good day a novice can easily hook up 20 trout, on a slow day a master will use all his skills to touch one fish. The fly fisher in tune with the Kamloops trout and its watery world can expect good action. The largest and most heavily fished lake in the area is the legendary Tunkwa Lake. Having an average depth of just 17 feet Tunkwa's entire area, approximately 300 hectares is capable of producing weed growth and in turn aquatic invertebrate. The calcium rich waters, a condition of all lakes, produce an abundance of freshwater shrimp which is a staple for the Kamloops trout. In an area renowned for its prolific chironomid hatches, Tunkwa's are the strongest. Despite the heavy pressure Tunkwa still produces trout exceeding 8lbs. Many smaller lakes fall into this category of high productivity although fish sizes are likely to be in the 2 - 4 lb range. The Tunkwa lake area is now being managed as a Provincial Park. Changes to usage, accessibility and fees are unknown for 1998. I do however believe these future changes will impact favorably on the fishery. Tunkwa Lake Resort will continue to offer both camping and cabins.

Higher elevation lakes typically have more deep water zones, greater competition for food and smaller fish. A notable exception is the popular Island Lake (Big O.K.). Having no natural spawning and regulated as the areas only catch and release fishery, this fly-only lake produces fish in the double digit weight class. A particularly strong sedge hatch can lead to some tremendous dry fly fishing. A large sunken island and deep water (35-40ft) zones at both the lakes north and south ends provide good structure throughout the open season. Presently, both Tunkwa and Island lakes experience heavy pressure especially on early season weekends. Fly fishers would be mistaken to only concentrate on these two lakes, as many other area lakes offer tremendous fly fishing opportunities.

As mentioned earlier, freshwater shrimp or scuds, are the staple food source. Shades of olive through brown and blue-grey are most common. Poking around shoreline rocks or weeds will always turn up a few specimens to help match size and color. Although scuds can be found throughout the water column, keeping your fly on the bottom will ensure greater success. Floating lines can be effective in depths to 6ft. Sink- tips or full sinking lines will be required for depths to 20 ft. Edges of weed beds, over weed carpets and rocky or gravely shoals (drop off zones, particularly in late summer) are all good scud habitat. Retrieve erratically (long slow, short fast) pausing frequently, don't straight line steady speed troll. The only effective way to troll any fly, especially in shallow water is from a float tube. Experienced oarsman may take exception, however, not holding both rod and fly line is a definite disadvantage. Back to scuds, an all round good size would be 12, although its not uncommon to find trout exclusively feeding on size 18 and smaller. Don't forget the bright orange brood pouch on pregnant females.

Early May in this area of the Thompson - Nicola can bring

some pretty technical chironomid fishing. Size 18 - 24 may be the order of the day. Exact color matches are crucial during the early season. Fishing smaller flies deeper (20 - 25ft) can make strikes difficult to detect. Most area chironomid fly fishers use floating lines, strike indicators, long leaders and split shot or weighted flies from an anchored boat. If bobber and sinker fishing seem like less than fly fishing, they can easily be eliminated. Weighted flies (bead heads work well) or fast sinking leaders and tippets will get the fly down quickly. Developing a keen sense of feel and concentration will accomplish all an indicator will, except in very deep water. Intermediate sinking lines give the angler direct contact with the fly, ensuring a high percentage of hookups, although limited to the top 6 - 8 feet of water. Density compensated sinking fly lines are invaluable when fishing chironomids in deep water, either crawled across the bottom or straight below an anchored position up through the water column. The idea is to simulate the chironomid pupae rise from the lakes bottom to the surface. Trout may be feeding at any point in the water column. Sinking line methods are best for determining that depth, while floating lines are great for keeping your fly in that zone. Of course, as the hatch progresses or wains, so to will the feeding zone. As the water warms in springtime chironomid activity increases. Size 12 - 14 are most common from June through September, although on some lakes size 8 may be dominate. Evening rises to adult chironomids, especially the larger ones are not uncommon after a warm sunny spring or early summer day. This is usually the first dry fly activity on many lakes, and though not fast and furious it can be quite rewarding. Try dark patterns matched to size, Tom Thumbs or Elk Hair Caddis for larger sizes, Midges or Griffiths Gnat for small offerings.

Chironomid larvae or bloodworms are fished in much the same manner as the pupae, except almost always on the bottom. Usually red in color, although often shades of green or olive. During spring or fall turnover larvae often come to the surface with bottom debris. Bloodworms will "wash up" from wave activity on windward shore areas becoming easy prey for trout. Often if chironomid pupae fishing slows, switching to bloodworm patterns can be productive. Much has been written on chironomid fishing in the Kamloops area. I would encourage anyone not familiar with the techniques to study all the information they can get their hands on, however the best educator is nature itself, just observe what's happening in and on the water and then imitate.

Of all aquatic insects, damsels and dragons are the least likely to be fished to their potential. Damsel flies spend a year or more as nymphs, dragons up to 4 or 5 years. Being hunters and stalkers they are often vulnerable to predation by trout. Although they are available year round as a food source and very active throughout the open water season, most fly fishers ignore them except during peak emergent periods. Immature nymphs are smaller, lighter in color and brighter, particularly after molting. Again, your fly should be on or near the bottom in 4 - 16 feet of water. A gravely bottom with some weed growth present seems preferable to immature damsel nymphs. They are slow but steady swimmers, pause to rest, or crawl about on cover. A favorite pattern is the Georgi Damsel. Tied almost entirely of sweet ginger marabou with grouse hackle and mono eyes on a 1x heavy size 12 hook, this fly has become essential on many area lakes. Thirty plus fish on the same fly has been reported several times. Whether you tie or buy flies, durability, by design and workmanship should be of prime concern. Lost time to changing worn flies or replacing shortened tippets, especially with cold fingers or low light levels can limit productivity on the water.

Barbless hooks (required by law on many lakes) will increase hookups due to better penetration. Although fish may be lost, usually when jumping and head shaking, tests show barbless hooks still bring more fish to hand. The real benefit to fishing barbless is ease of release. Limited handling and the ability to release trout without removing them from the water goes a long way to reducing the mortality rate of a released fish, especially larger overplayed trout or those in a spawning condition. Self release or unhooking your fishing partner are an added bonus to fishing barbless.

Peak emergent periods for damsel flies start in early June and last through July. Nymphs swim to within inches of the surface then slowly make their way to the shore line or weed beds to climb up onto any protruding vegetation. It's as the damsels approach these areas that the trout key in. Floating lines with size 10, 2x or 3x, flies matched to color bring spectacular strikes. Be prepared to up your tippet strength and resist the temptation to strike back. Both dragonfly species, Darners and Gomphus should also be fished deep. Although the more common Darner is a fast swimmer, both patterns are more effective fished at a crawl. A sporatic rapid retrieve may be incorporated, especially should it prove effective.

Without a doubt leeches account for more big trout than any other pattern. Again, stay on the bottom. Evening and Autumn days are the best times to fish in 6 ft or less of water. Through the spring and summer season 6 - 12 feet seems to be the most effective depth. The key to successful leech fishing is keep them small during daylight hours. Size 10 is about right, although 12's and 14's are often productive for big fish. Retrieves vary from as fast as possible to a crawl. Experimenting is the only way to determine an effective retrieve on a given day. Maroon is a favorite color, although olive, brown and black are also effective. Any type of dubbed fur or synthetic body with a short marabou tail makes a attractive pattern. A bit of Krystal Flash added to the tail or wound through the body makes a good all-round attractor pattern. When looking for trout on a slow day try trolling or troll and strip these small flashy patterns from a float tube. The relatively recent use of bead heads on still water flies adds weight, flash and a tantalizing undulating motion to a leech pattern. Larger leeches (up to 4 inches long) should be reserved for night fishing. Troll shallow areas with a floating line, cast from shore or casting from an anchored position.

Far more has been written about mayflies than you'll ever need to know when fishing our area lakes. Although prolific hatches still occur on larger or more out of the way lakes, sporatic at best is all too common. The use of outboards, particularly 2 strokes have all but wiped out mayflies, and a to lesser extent caddis fly populations in many of our lakes. It seems incredible to me that filtering exhaust gases and releasing unburned lubricating oils into our lakes is tolerated. Oils collect on the lakes surface and eventually settle on the shoreline areas. This is known as the bathtub ring effect. It is these shoreline areas that are the habitat for mayfly nymphs and sedge larvae. Our lakes are small and being in a semiarid climate, little flushing occurs. This of course contributes to a lakes productivity by containing nutrients. Unfortunately pollutants are also contained. Studies show dissolved hydro carbons weaken immune and reproductive systems in trout. All that aside, trolling small lakes with gas outboards rates as the least effective method of taking trout. Outboards, however, are often required on larger wind swept lakes for safety reasons. Most lakes still have caddis fly hatches to some degree, however, the real prolific caddis hatches are found on difficult or recent access lakes.

Hatches begin from mid June to mid July, depending on elevation. Whether fishing pupae or adults on the surface, this is the best fly fishing that B.C. has to offer. Patience and nerve are required as large trout chase down and attempt to drown dry offerings before taking them. Hatches can last for weeks, usually mid-morning although any time day or night is not uncommon. Female sedges returning to lay eggs bring trout to the surface through late summer. Water boatman patterns can be effective during and immediately after ice-off. Again in late September and October during boatman and backswimmer egg laying flights, trout will key on these air breathing insects. Terrestrials are not that important except at times when black Flying Ants cover a lakes surface.

Wildlife abounds. Deer, moose and Black Bear are abundant throughout the area. Ospreys and Eagles demonstrate their unique fishing techniques while Humming birds and Whiskey Jacks entertain campers. Various song birds and waterfowl make our lakes their summer home. Lynx, Bobcat, and Cougar are indigenous but rarely seen. Most nights Coyotes and Owls keep things from getting too quiet.

I find it disturbing when I read articles describing methods and areas to angle for trout as they prepare to spawn. These fish though large, offer little sport when hooked and suffer a high mortality rate when released due to their already stressed condition. If retained they make poor quality table fare. In B.C. it is unlawful to fish within 100 meters of a spawning channel. All anglers are encouraged to use the observe, record, report program described in the Freshwater Fishing Synopsis or contact a Conservation Officer or the R.C.M.P.

Logan Lake is a community of about 2,700. All amenities are available including lodging and camping. Several forestry sites are located on nearby lakes, perfect for rustic or R.V. camping. Resorts are featured on a limited number of lakes, reservations are recommended. For more information on visiting this area please contact the Logan Lake Chamber of Commerce at (250) 523-6504.

Steve Jennings

Born in 1949, Steve Jennings started coarse fishing in England when he was 8 years old. Ten years later a friend introduced him to reservoir fly fishing and he has been a committed fly angler ever since. Steve emigrated to Canada in 1971. The only things he brought from the Old Country were a few clothes and his fly rods. He still lives in the log house he built in 1978 with his wife Darlene, daughter Mikala, and son Matthew.

In 1990 he opened Little Fort Fly and Tackle in downtown Little Fort and can be found there most days from May to October when he isn't out guiding or just fishing for fun. Recently Steve has fulfilled a lifelong dream of fly fishing on a year round basis, he is involved in a lodge project in Central America where in the winter months he helps clients catch bonefish and tarpon.

Copies of A Fly fisher's Guide to the Nehalliston Lakes and A Fly fisher's Guide to the Interlakes and 100 Mile Area can be purchased from Little Fort Fly and Tackle, Box 75, Little Fort, B.C., V0E-2C0 or call/fax (250) 677-4366.

Littlefort and the Rainbow Highway
Steve Jennings

I didn't get to the lake until 6:30, it had been a frustrating day, the log house I was building had been fighting me, nothing major, just little stuff not going my way. I was glad when the log I had struggled with for an hour slid into place and my wife said "Why don't you go fishing honey?".

The year was 1978 and 6:30 pm isn't a bad time to start fishing if it's June 21st, solstice, the longest day of the year. The road to the Emar lakes was, at that time, a dusty, bumpy grind with a little 4X4 at the end, the new Highway 24 was just a plan. I carried my boat to Boulder Lake from the end of the road, rowed across Boulder, then a short portage and I was there, Club Lake. Club was mirror calm and the bugs were bad. I hate using repellent but these guys would pick my bones clean if I didn't. So far the spring of '78 had been a wet one, but today had been hot and sunny and I was hoping that the sedge hatch would be on. The mosquitos followed me for a while but lost enthusiasm as I neared the center of the lake. Not a ripple or rise broke the calm, you would have thought this was a barren lake, but that angler's sixth sense was working overtime and I knew that this was just a waiting game.

****

The Interior of British Columbia was truly a fly fisher's paradise. Those of us fortunate enough to carve out a living far away from the big city had an abundance of choices, hundreds of lakes and some great rivers. Kamloops was at the centre of it all, Kamloops trout became famous for their fight and tenacity, the fly fisher who figured out the hatch could fill the boat. If you saw another boat on the lake you would row over and say "Hi" and compare notes on where the action was. Long weekends would see a few guys up from the coast, braving the twists and turns of the Fraser Canyon for that precious time on the trout lakes. Each spring brought the anticipation of a new season, a time to use the knowledge and observations gleaned from last year. You thought that these wonderful fisheries could only get better. Then it suddenly changed when (then) Premier Bill Bennet drove a car through a banner for the opening of the Coquihalla Highway. In a mere 3 1/2 hours an angler could finish tying a fly in his Surrey home and cast that very fly on a Merritt lake. The pressure on the lakes increased almost overnight. Instead of rowing over to another boat to chat, you now had problems finding enough room to launch. I remember great days on Peterhope Lake, twitching a chironomid, the outlet shoal all to myself, silver missiles launching when the hook sank into the snout tissue, my leader trailing behind. I also remember in 1987 returning for a nostalgia trip, fifty boats on the lake, dogs running loose, dirt bikes, portable generators, Peterhopeless. Then Brad Pitt stood on a rock in a Montana river, shadow casting. A River Runs Through It rang up the numbers at the box office and ran up the numbers of new fly anglers. Fly fishing went ballistic, but the silver missiles became harder to find.

However, just an hour's drive north of Kamloops, in the beautiful North Thompson Valley, you find Little Fort. "Blink and you miss it" is an apt description, but time has been kind to this little village, and not much has changed here. Little Fort has an important junction at it's heart for here is the beginning of highway 24. Not a long road, just 109 km. From this link between Highway 5 and 97, you can access more trout lakes than anywhere else in B.C. Highway 24 is the Rainbow Highway.

Two distinct areas can be identified along this road. From Little Fort there is a steep climb just a couple of kilometers from town, an 8% grade for 8 km puts you near the top of the Nehalliston Plateau. This is a float tuber's paradise, over one hundred lakes to choose, many walk-in only, small lakes each with something a little different to offer. The largest lake on the plateau is Taweel at 1600 acres and some of the smallest are 4 or 5 acres, just potholes, but some of these have huge trout, not always easy to catch but surprisingly big for such a small body of water.

As you drop down from the plateau heading west the highway passes Lac Des Roches and this is the beginning of the Interlakes area. Lac Des Roches is the first of what is called "the big three", the other two are Bridge Lake and Sheridan Lake. These large lakes produce trophy sized trout. Many rainbows over 10 lbs are caught each season. Bridge Lake is also known for it's huge kokanee that will readily take nymphs and streamers and have been known to gulp dry flies from the surface. A couple of weeks after ice off much fun can be had casting to cruising lake trout in the shallows,

Hike-in fishing can be very beautiful

when the water warms they go deep, so it's just a brief opportunity to catch yet another species on the fly. Sheridan Lake has great rainbow trout fishing and also has Eastern Brook trout that grow to 5 lbs and better. When a falling barometer puts the rainbows into a funk, the brookies can go into a feeding frenzy, so there's never a dull moment on Sheridan.

Although the big three dominate the map, there are plenty of great fisheries both north and south of the highway, many of them have become classic fly fishing waters known only to a few locals who will not tell you how good they really are. Who can blame them for wanting to keep such fishing a secret for a few more years.

To describe in detail every lake in these two areas would take a book thicker than War and Peace, but there's a certain excitement in discovering new waters and having a written account of every hot spot may take away from the joy of discovery.

I have put together two maps covering these two areas. A Fly fisher's Guide to the Nehalliston Lakes gives an easy to read map showing 125 lakes with a brief written description of each one. A Fly fisher's Guide to the Interlakes and 100 Mile Area shows all the lakes important to the fly angler with detailed depth charts of the big three.

The landscape of these two areas is very different. The Nehalliston is a wooded plateau, pine and spruce being the dominant species. Lakes here are a mixture of darker, tea colored water and clear, blue water with marl shoals. The fish in the more acidic lakes tend to be a little slower growing and have more of a brassy hue, the colors and markings are more pronounced with red fins, a deep rose sideband and heavy spotting on the back and tail. Trout from marl lakes are more silver with light spotting. These almost look like two different species but it's really just an adaptation to their environment and food sources by the same fish. The important point is that the fight is the same, streaking runs with many aerial displays that have the reel singing and the heart pounding.

The Nehalliston Lakes are not for big boats, there are no launching ramps and for the most part motors are not necessary. Cartoppers and canoes give good access but the real tool for these lakes is a float tube or pontoon boat. Many of these lakes are managed as walk-in fisheries and are impossible to fish from shore, the trails are wide enough to carry your inflated float tube and you can always find a solid bottom from which to launch. Mobility is crucial in the Nehalliston, if one lake is off the next one can be hot and there are lots to choose from.

There is a definite change of scenery when you drop off the Nehalliston Plateau into the Interlakes area. Open grasslands with stands of Lodgepole Pine and Aspen, surround most of the lakes. The terrain is flatter, with most of the lakes of the blue water type with vast marl shoals and reed beds. The larger lakes have launching ramps. But of course not every boat launched is a fishing craft, be aware that during the hot days of summer the water sport enthusiasts will drive the fly fisher away to seek quieter waters. But the spring, fall and evenings belong to the fly fisher on the big lakes (and the hatches are big too!). When the ice comes off it all starts with the chironomids, they range in size and color from a tiny lime green size 18 to the huge copper brown at nearly an inch long. Catch your first fish and get out your stomach pump, the sample will show you two of the three factors of successful chironomid fishing, size and color. Find the depth at which the trout are feeding and you're in for a day to remember. Keep checking with that stomach pump throughout the day as some hatches fade others will take over. Of course you never have the exact fly you need, and a midge hatch will show up the gaps in your fly box. Here's a few you should have: bloodworms in red, maroon and olive sizes 12-16, chironomids in lime green with black head sizes 16 & 18, black with silver rib sizes 14-16, brown with copper rib sizes 10-14, and silver-gray with dark red rib sizes 14-16.

As the season progresses into May and June look for Callibaetis mayfly hatches. Watch for birds such as swallows and terns swooping in for the feast and often you will also see the trout sipping at the little grey "sailboats" from below. For the nymph, try Hare's Ears or Pheasant Tails sizes 14-16 fished just subsurface with a long leader on a floating or intermediate line. The dry fly that has brought me the most success is the Grey Wulff size 12, it floats so well, with it's elk hair wings and tail, that once dressed (and with a couple of air drying false casts between fish), it can out last most other patterns for floatability.

I remember a few years ago having a banner day on Lac Des Roches, it was May 18th 1992 and a warm spring followed a very mild winter. I was driving to another lake when I saw a group of terns working one of the shoals of the big lake. I stopped the truck and watched through field glasses as trout by the hundreds attacked a cloud of mayflies. By the time I got rigged up a strong west

71

wind had come up and the lake was rough with a three foot wave pattern scouring the shoal. Cursing my luck I almost quit before I started, then the morning sun shone through the crest of each wave silhouetting masses of nymphing trout. Using a long leader and a Hare's Ear nymph all I had to do was let the fly drift in the wave tops. The first take broke the tippet, then the same thing happened to the replacement fly. Stepping up to 8lb. tippet from 4lb. made a difference with my next cast, a beautiful 3lb Blackwater rainbow with it's razor sharp teeth came to the net and showed me why I was breaking fish off. I took a dozen more of similar size on the nymph then the wind suddenly stopped and just as suddenly the action switched to dry mayflies as thousands of insects emerged taking advantage of the lull. My size 12 Grey Wulff was engulfed first cast and another Blackwater danced on his tail as I set the hook. Trout were sipping mayflies all around me and I could see no other angler on the lake. The calm conditions lasted for only half an hour and with a roar the wind returned and, as if a switch had been thrown, the mays stopped hatching and the nymph came into play again. I caught and released over 50 fish that day.

From the middle of June and on into July is the time for the big caddis hatches. Known as the Travelling sedge, these are the heavyweights of the dry fly world. With naturales measuring up to two inches it's time to get out your big deer hair flies such as the Mikaluk Sedge or size 6 Tom Thumb and wake them like steelhead dries. When a hatch is in full swing it seems that you can't get it out there fast enough. The rises are, in a word, explosive and some of the largest fish in the lakes are up and looking for the big insects. If surface action is spotty, go deeper with sedge pupa patterns. A green Carey Special is a good fly to try as a searching fly.

At about the same time of year the lakes with reedy edges have a tremendous damsel fly emergence. A pale green Whitty Damsel Nymph cast to the trembling reeds can bring great rewards if you can turn the trout away from the reeds before they break your tippet.

Dragonfly nymphs are abundant in both areas, my favorite method is to use my type 4 sinking line, a short stubby leader of 2-5 feet long and "walk" deer hair patterns, in either Darner size (4's and 6's) or Gomphus (in 8 or 10), along the bottom. Avoid a steady retrieve as you will bury the fly in the weeds, try a couple of tugs then an eight second pause, it will keep the buoyant fly just above the weeds. The take is often so violent that a rod can be pulled from your hands, and yet other times they seem to just "lean" on the fly and feel like a hookup with an old log, until you set the hook and all hell breaks loose.

Leeches are to be found in all the lakes and are probably the best way to search the water when no definite hatch is obvious. Two of the best are the Little Fort Leech with its distinctive red slash and bottle green crystal chenille, and the sparse Mohair Blood Leech in fuchia or burgundy.

Late July, all of August and early September can see the lakes at the lower elevations slow down as the water warms. Now is the time to seek the high lakes at over 4,000 feet where the water is cooler and the hatches more spread out. This also is the time when the three main trout rivers that are close by, the Clearwater, Mahood and Canim are at their most fishable. The freshet is over and there is nothing finer on a hot day than wading a shady, cool river casting both dries and nymphs into a myriad of likely looking spots. With catch and release restrictions these rivers are making a comeback and rainbows to 5 lbs are found in all three.

The spring of 1997 had been cool and damp and all the hatches were three weeks behind where they usually were. This situation carried over into the summer and although it played havoc with timing for lake hatches, it had a most amazing effect on the Canim River. With a road closure (due to flooding) cutting off the Mahood River, which is my usual choice for opening day, I arrived at the Canim with my son Matthew (who loves fishing rivers more than anything else except perhaps playing hockey). Normally opening day (July 1st) on the Canim you can find remnants of the stone fly's egg laying surface action that usually peaks in mid June. The hatch delay had carried over with the stone flies too. The trees and rocks at the river bank were festooned with the shucked skins of thousands of nymphs that had recently crawled out of the river. The air was filled with the black and orange females alighting on the river to deposit their eggs and the trout were going nuts. Matt waded out to a large rock that split the flow into two seams, tucking himself in the lee of the rock he was able to alternate casts between these seams and for an hour he caught a fish almost every cast. The big Improved Sofa Pillow he was using only had to slap the water a second or two when another trout grabbed it and danced for him. I just stood and watched, a proud dad watching his kid have fun.

In mid September something magical happens, the nights get cold enough to produce the first frosts but the days still have warmth with that nice flat light. It's Indian Summer and the backswimmer mating flights get the trout into a feeding mood. As the sun reaches it's zenith, look for drifting little puff balls that in an instant disappear with a raindrop-like plop that marks the insect's transition from airborne traveller to aquatic oarsman. These flights can go on for weeks and usually last all day with the trout crashing the surface, often chasing down individual insects with a dogged determination. My favorite fly is of my own creation, with a foam body and rubber legs, the Jennings Ultimate Boatman took years of trial and error, but it is unbeatable when the flight is on. On one of those trial days I took my friend Bob McCullough for his first outing in a float tube. He had recently moved to Sheridan Lake after retiring from the Coast Guard, his last posting, at Ucluelet, had given him the opportunity to fish for salmon whenever he liked but it had been a few years since he had fly fished for trout. We arrived at Irish Lake just outside the town of Lone Butte, a nice little lake kept productive with a couple of aerators that have eliminated the winter kill that plagued Irish for years. We started hanging chironomids on long leaders and I caught a couple of fish around a pound and a half, Bob switched to a blood leech and had a couple of bumps. At 11:00 am, the air was still, the sun broke through and the lake started to boil with trout rising to backswimmers drifting in like a cloud. Quickly I kicked over to Bob and gave him one of my experimental boatman patterns, I told him to cast to the rise and twitch the fly on the surface. As I was rigging up the same fly on a slow sinking outfit, Bob let out a whoop as a large, chrome rainbow nailed his fly on his second cast. He kept this fish, swearing that his wife would never believe him unless he took one home for dinner. Before I could take my first cast he was into another one bigger than the three pounder he had just killed. It took a lot of persuading to get him to release that fish, an old saltchucker like Bob was not used to putting them back. When the surface action slowed my sinking line came into play and I caught and released (much to Bob's dismay) fish after fish, pulling the fly down with short, fast strips perfectly imitating the diving backswimmers. I ended the day with around thirty fish and Bob, with a dozen, said it was the best day's trout fishing he had ever experienced. A few days later I returned to Irish and the fishing was just the same, at midday the lake turned on and the same foam boatman did its magic all over again.

As fall progresses look to the shrimp patterns, both Gammarus and Hyalella, to take fish as insects become scarce and the trout try to "bulk up" for the coming winter. The olive Baggy Shrimp in size 18 for Hyalella and size 10-14 for Gammarus. The days of October see the chironomid at the forefront again, even with ice forming at the fringes of the lakes, look for strong hatches and fat trout sipping them down before the curtain descends for another season.

Visitors can find a range of accommodations along highway 24 from the motels in Little Fort and 100 Mile House to Bed & Breakfast in some really unique homes. The ultimate is to stay at one of the many lake side fishing resorts, there's one to suit every taste and pocket book. Some offer a full "American Plan" with cabins, meals, boats and the trimmings at a fixed daily rate. Others offer the look-after-yourself approach with house keeping cabins and boat rentals by the hour or the day. Whichever you choose you will find that the folks who run them are friendly and dedicated to making sure you have a good time regardless of your skills as an angler or whatever the weather conditions. Unfortunately these people are a dying breed, with high taxation and poor support from government agencies many are calling it quits and resorts are closing their doors to the public and becoming the property of the rich or private syndicates. The rule is to book ahead a year in advance to get the best times or at least call around before you arrive to avoid disappointment. Of course there's always camping, many of the Nehalliston Lakes have forest recreation sites, camping is free but other than a pit toilet and a picnic table there are no facilities. Bridge Lake has a Provincial campground and many of the resorts have hookups and space reserved for the angler who's home is on wheels.

Clear-cut logging has few advantages as far as tourism is concerned, but one of these advantages is that habitat for wildlife is opened up providing tender new growth for moose, deer and black bear to browse upon and these animals are abundant. Waterfowl are also plentiful, and in the case of Loons, too plentiful. On some lakes loons will wait for a fish to be hooked then try to steal it before it can be brought to the net, a real nuisance. As for raptors, Bald Headed Eagles and Osprey will give you impressive lessons on how to catch fish.

Highway 24 is now complete, the last unpaved section was

capped in 1995. With the exception of Lac Des Roches you only get glimpses of a few of the lakes from the road. The Rainbow Highway will give you a smooth ride and access so many lakes that they are never really crowded, if you don't want to share a lake you can always find solitude.

In recent years committees of resource users have formed to preserve the unique qualities of the area. Logging is still taking place, but now it is done with some sensitivity to the needs of the recreationalist. A preservation plan that allows resource extraction with the emphasis on restoring the landscape to as close as it was before the trees were felled. If a lake was walk-in before logging took place it is returned to that status as soon as possible afterwards.

Catch and gear restrictions have been instituted to preserve some of the smaller, sensitive lakes. Local anglers have come to realize that this is a unique area and have donated time and money to projects like the Grizzly Anglers spawning channel on Lac Des Roches and the Friends of Sheridan Lake's two spawning enhancement projects. With a little care and attention the Rainbow Highway will shine for years to come.

****

As the sun dipped on Club Lake I had used the time in waiting to tie six large Tom Thumbs to pieces of tippet with loop to loop connections. I stuck the flies in a line along the gunnel of the boat, I wanted a quick change if the action heated up and the light faded. The first indication of fish movement was a loud splash behind me. I whirled around to see a fluttering sedge engulfed by the trout's second attempt at getting it's dinner. Close by another sedge was popping from its skin, it's adulthood lasted but the blink of an eye before it too disappeared in a violent explosion of golden water. I fired out a Tom Thumb, it hit the water only inches from the epicenter of the explosion. The fly sat for a second before another eruption tightened the line in my hand. I was prepared for this violent take and the tippet parted with an audible crack. A huge trout broke the water in three successive leaps, my Tom Thumb and trailing tippet clearly visible and I reached down for the first of my replacements.

I came back to reality when I slid my hand along the gunnel to find I had no more "bullets" left, it was very dark, my arms ached from playing trout, I couldn't see my watch but I knew it was late. The slurping and splashing was still going on as I pulled up the anchor and headed for shore. I still had to portage, row across Boulder Lake, find my truck, forty minutes of driving to get home and another log on my house to struggle with tomorrow. I was really tired, but a good tired.

British Columbia's Region 8

The lakes of the Okanagan are very similar to the lakes of the Cariboo. Very rich in aquatic life and teeming with large rainbow trout. The most attractive aspect of angling in region 8 is that you don't have to leave the family at home. With many water sports and other recreational activities it can be a trip the whole family enjoys. Large lakes like Okanagan, Mable and Skaha can offer fair fishing and Okanagan Lake has some great beaches. Mable is the best fishing out of the large lakes. Kalamalka and Wood attract anglers looking for those tasty Kokanee. So many good lakes and general good weather make this an excellent stillwater destination.

Known more for the many lakes, streams like the Kettle and Granby can be overlooked, which is fine if you spend a fair bit of time there. Fly fishing is a very effective form of fishing in this region. Kamloops trout come to the fly very well and with lakes so abundant in feed, trophies are just waiting to be caught.

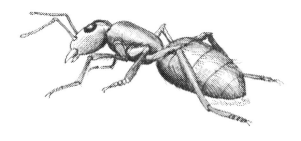

Raul Poole

For the last twenty years Raul Poole has spent much of his summers fly fishing the waters of B.C. and Alberta. These days, when he's not fishing himself, he spends his summer days guiding clients to the best spots on the Kettle and some of his other favorite rivers. He lives and works in Rock Creek, B.C. with his wife and two children where he operates the tour company, Drifters Rod "N" River Adventures. If your looking for a guided trip, he may be contacted at 250-446-2442.

The Wild Kettle River

Raul Poole

It's true, I'll admit it. I'm one of those guys who has run around a lot in the past. It's hard to say exactly why I acted the way I did. I guess it was mostly because I was young and slightly restless, and also a whole lot less experienced than I am now. I think that I must have wanted to be sure that I wasn't missing something special that might have been happening someplace else by staying at home. This tendency to stray might not have been so hard to understand were it not for the fact that the whole time I had everything most people ever could have wanted right in my own backyard.

Yes, there was once a time when I would spend an unhealthy amount of my time (unhealthy according to my wife) racing around from one river to the next, trying to coordinate my arrivals with the best fishing conditions of the year. The giant Salmon fly hatch on the Crowsnest, the enormous hatches of Green Drakes on the Upper Skagit, the legendary Traveling sedges of the Kamloops area lakes, and the first run of fall coho on the Bella Coola are just a few examples of the sort of places that I would regularly tear off to at a moments notice, forsaking family, friends, and loved ones, in order to pursue fish that, as often as not, were completely unimpressed with my offerings. When I look through some of my past fishing journals, they sometimes seem more like the log of some sort of crazed rally car driver from hell than the diaries of someone who wanted to do nothing more noble than snag a fish or two with a hook that was made to look like something else with bits of feather and animal hair.

Although it's true that I did have some great fishing days and some wonderful experiences during those years, the fact is that when a person travels from place to place expecting to find the absolute best fishing conditions, more often than not they will be disappointed. Fly fishing in B.C. is a pass time that is far too dependent on the foreseeable whims of mother nature to be easily predictable. While it's true that I still like to go on fishing trips three or four times a year, these days I spend a whole lot more time kicking around on my home stream, the Kettle River, than I do anyplace else. I have learned that it is better, and often more productive, to know two or three rivers like the proverbial back of your hand, than it is to know a dozen or two places just enough to get by with. And it's not that I feel forsaken either, when it comes to my obsession with fly fishing for trout, I have trouble thinking of many other places I'd rather spend a day than drifting down one of my favorite stretches of the Kettle.

The Kettle River begins its trip to the ocean by tumbling out of the mountains and highlands that lie to the east of the Okanagan valley in southern British Columbia. It flows gin clear as it passes through forested hills, grasslands and ranch country. From there the river flows southwards until it crosses the U.S. border at the village of Midway; it then turns east and meanders through the semiarid farmland of northern Washington until it re-enters Canada at the town of Grand Forks. Here the Kettle meets it's major tributary, the Grandby, another excellent river for fly fishing. The much larger river then flows east another twenty or so miles, until it leaves Canada for good, near the town of Christina Lake. The creator must have had fly fishing in mind when the Kettle was created, because throughout its entire length in Canada, some 120 miles, its firm freestone bottom and its wonderful mix of riffles, pools, and runs provide an endless variety of opportunities to those of us who enjoy the challenge of chasing wild trout with what we hope are the right flies.

When your talking about fishing the Kettle River, as with almost all rivers in this part of the world, your talking about fishing for rainbow trout. They are the only trout that are native to the rivers of this area, and of all the trout species, they are best suited to the conditions here. However, over the last several decades there have been attempts by both the B.C. and Washington State governments to introduce populations of other trout into the system. Although overall these stocking efforts have not done particularly well, they were not completely unsuccessful either, and as a result, small residual populations of these fish remain. A good day on the Kettle could mean that not only would a person catch their fill of rainbows, but also a brookie or two, and maybe even a brown trout as well.

As with almost all freestones, most of the fish in the Kettle are on the smaller side of the fourteen inch mark. The forces that create rivers like these also create conditions for trout to live long enough to get much bigger than that; mostly because they have been cleaned out by fishermen during the vulnerable late summer low water periods when water temperatures and lack of stream cover kept the fish confined to a few small portions of the river. During these times, many people fishing the river either didn't realize the impact they were having on the fish population or just weren't concerned about it. In the past few years, several wetter summers in a row, combined with improved forestry and agricultural practices in the region, and a new concern for conservation among people fishing the river, who are releasing more fish than ever, have resulted in an noticeable increase in the numbers of fish being caught. Best of all, not only have the numbers of fish been on the increase, the numbers of large fish being caught, say over 20 inches has increased as well.

The Kettle River is the sort of place that supports populations of most of the aquatic insects that a person might hear about in fly fishing circles. In the late spring and early summer of each year there are sizable hatches of most of the various species of mayflies, stone flies and caddis flies that are popular among fishermen in the west. The main difference between the Kettle and some of the more famous western rivers is that rarely are the hatches of any one insect there heavy enough or long enough to cause the fish to become overly selective in their feeding habits. While it is always a good idea to pay attention to what's going on in the air and water around you when your fly fishing this river or anywhere else, on the Kettle "matching the hatch" rarely means more than selecting a fly with the correct size and silhouette and presenting it in a convincing manner. On this river, proper presentation is far more important than making the right choice of fly. The fish in the Kettle are true opportunists and more often than not they are willing to strike at anything that comes their way and looks good to eat.

During the last half of summer, Kettle River trout depend heavily on terrestrial insects as a source of food. At this time big fish will often hold in the protected lies that are close to stream side vegetation and wait for whatever sort of insects happen to fall into the current. Fly patterns that represent ants, beetles, and crickets will all be good producers. But for me this time of the year is hopper season, the best time of the year to go trout fishing. The grasslands surrounding the Kettle support large numbers of fat, juicy grasshoppers that trout love to gobble down. There is nothing I enjoy doing more in late summer than spending the afternoon wading the edges of the river, making my way upstream, and casting big hopper imitations into all the likely looking feeding places. At times like these, the fish are so crazed by what I like to call "hopper-mania" that often a sloppy cast that brings the fly down onto the water with an audible "splat" will have the best results.

My gear for these outings is as simple as I can possibly make it, which is a big part of what makes the whole experience so pleasurable. Heavy neoprene waders, fishing vests brimming with extra junk for all possible occasions, expensive felt soled wading boots, and clumsy landing nets are all left behind. My fishing attire consists of a T-shirt, shorts, and an old pair of tennis shoes. My extra fishing gear consists of one spool of tippet that is stuffed into the pocket of my shorts and a half dozen spare flies (all hoppers) stuck to the brim of my hat. The greatest thing about fishing this way is not only is it simple, pleasant and fun but it works! In all my years on the Kettle, the biggest fish I have caught there have been during hopper season.

After the spring freshet ends and the water levels have dropped and cleared, around mid June most years, the Kettle River is best suited to using lighter tackle and gear. My favorite setups for this time of year are 9 foot, 4 or 5 weight rods combined with a full floating line and a 10 to 12 foot leader. My personal preference is to fish the current seams and pocket water using dry flies, but a nymph that is dead drifted close to the bottom at the heads of pools and riffles can be a great producer as well. Best bet for dry flies include Elk Hair Caddis in sizes   14 - 18, gnats and other midge imitations in sizes 18 - 22, and my all time favorite trout fishing dry fly, a black bodied size 14 Tom Thumb.

When nymphing, I like to start out the season using larger sized stone fly imitations to represent the Golden stone flies and Giant Salmon flies that are coming off at this time. By mid July when the Stone flies are pretty much done for the year, I usually find that caddis larva imitations and Bead Head Pheasant Tails work best. When nymph fishing in the Kettle, or any other stream for that matter, it is important to remember that the fish will most often hold very close to, if not right on, the stream bottom where the current is less strong and the feed is most concentrated. The most common mistake that many inexperienced fishermen make is that they fail to get their fly close enough to the stream bottom to attract the fish's attention and it drifts harmlessly above the fish. For this reason, I always suggest that people use nymphs which are tied with a few turns of lead wire attached to the hook shank to act as a weight. Also, a few small split shot weights attached to your tippet 6 or so inches from the fly, is a sure fire way to get your rig to the bottom in a hurry.

Fishing season for trout on the Kettle usually begins around mid June and continues through till about the end of October. During summer, the water temperature can be high enough that the fish become sluggish during the hottest parts of the day. Above the settlement of Westbridge, where the West Kettle and the Main Kettle rivers meet, the are a series of excellent Forestry Recreational campsites spread out at different scenic sites along the main river. There is also a popular provincial campground on the river situated eight kilometers upstream from the settlement of Rock Creek which many people use as a base camp for day long fishing trips. Single or multiple day guided float trips on the Kettle River, plus other waters in the area can be arranged through Drifters Rod 'N River Adventures, based in Rock Creek B.C.

Sipping trout and the evening rise

Chironomid Emerger

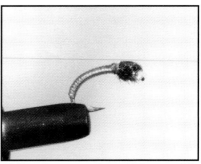

Olive Swannundaze Chironomid

Black Swannundaze Chironomid

Bead Head Chironomid

Standard Thread Chironomid

Glass Bead Head Chironomid

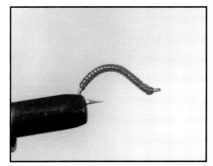

Red Bloodworm

Bead Head Emerger

Trout Flies Tied By Jeff Mironuck

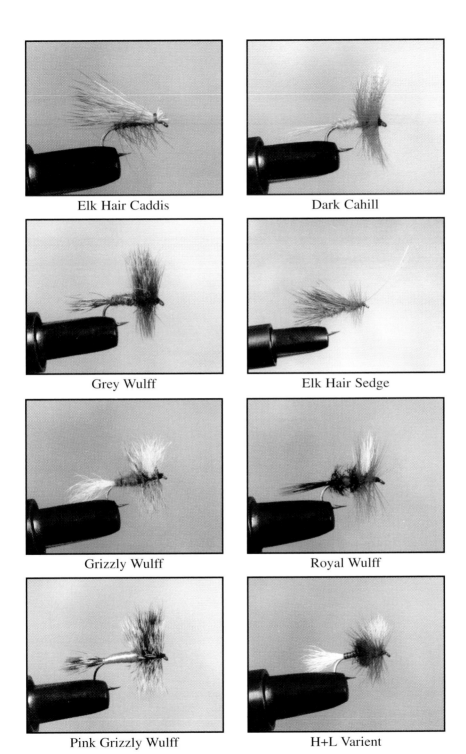

Elk Hair Caddis

Dark Cahill

Grey Wulff

Elk Hair Sedge

Grizzly Wulff

Royal Wulff

Pink Grizzly Wulff

H+L Varient

Trout Flies Tied By Jeff Mironuck

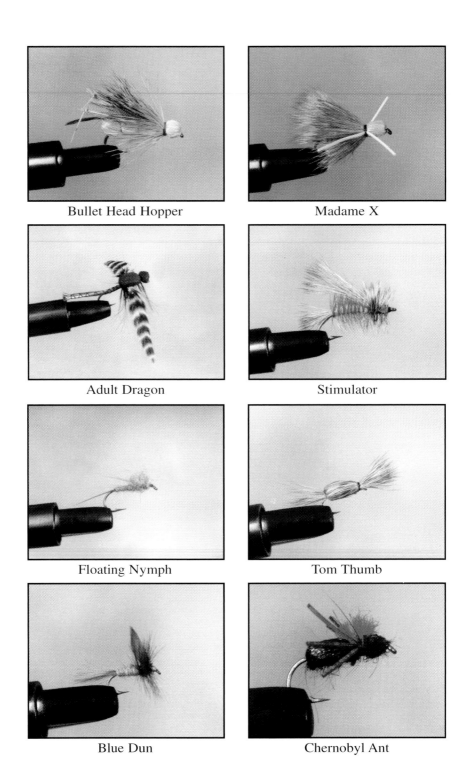

Bullet Head Hopper

Madame X

Adult Dragon

Stimulator

Floating Nymph

Tom Thumb

Blue Dun

Chernobyl Ant

Trout Flies Tied By Jeff Mironuck

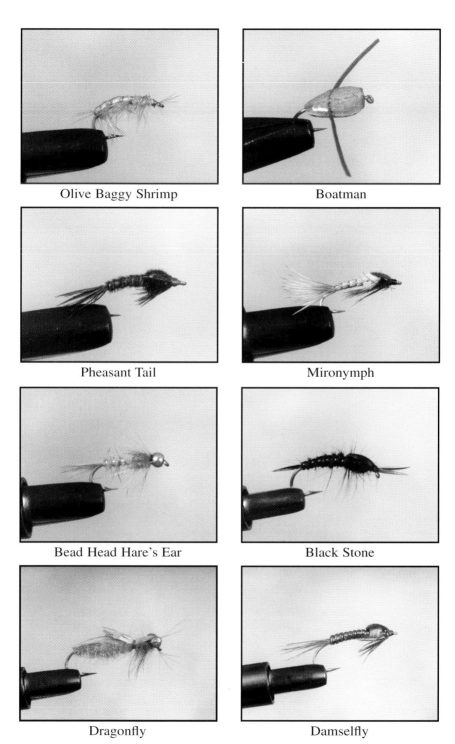

Olive Baggy Shrimp

Boatman

Pheasant Tail

Mironymph

Bead Head Hare's Ear

Black Stone

Dragonfly

Damselfly

Trout Flies Tied By Jeff Mironuck

Muddler Minnow

Bow River Bugger

Zonker

Egg Sucking Leech

Floating the Elk River in the south east corner of B.C.
Photo by David Lambroughton

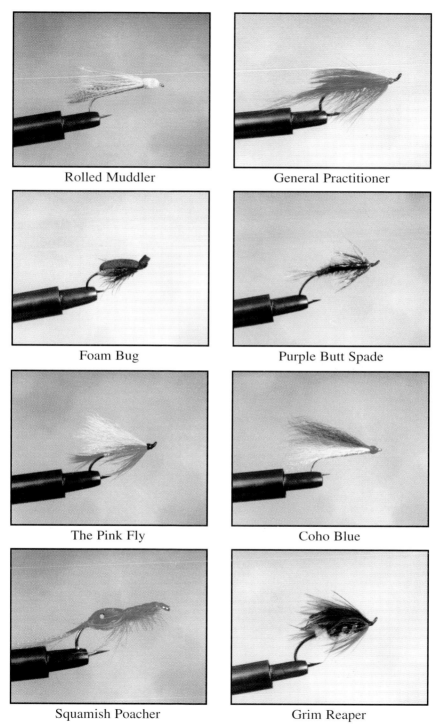

Rolled Muddler

General Practitioner

Foam Bug

Purple Butt Spade

The Pink Fly

Coho Blue

Squamish Poacher

Grim Reaper

Steelhead and Salmon flies supplied by Michael and Young

Sunset on the Bow River

British Columbia's Region 4

Thanks to the many dams in the Columbia River drainage anglers in region 4 never get the thrill of fighting salmon or steelhead. Bordered by Alberta and the U.S., region 4 has countless remote areas where anglers seldom visit. Rainbows, and cutthroat are the prized possession of fly fishers in the Kootenays and waters like the Elk, Columbia, St.Mary and Kootenay Lake attract much attention. Kootenay lake holds huge rainbows and Dollies that run upwards of 20 pounds. The cutthroat in this region are very common and fishing can be great in the smallest of trickles. With equal opportunities for lake and river fishing, region 4 is truly a trout fishers paradise.

In the west, The Upper and Lower Arrow lakes have gained quite a reputation for trophy Gerrard rainbow fishing. Like the similar Kootenay Lake, trolling buck tails and other tackle is the preferred method. Duck Lake near Creston is one of the top bass lakes in B.C. Many surrounding lakes also hold good numbers of these fish and fly fishing for them can be very exciting. Countless smaller deep cold lakes abound in the Kootenay region. With very little pressure and some good angling opportunities it's the perfect place to get away from the crowds.

Steve Harris

Living in the Kootenays for most of his life has given Steve Harris the opportunity to perfect his stillwater skills on the many pristine lakes. He is currently employed with the school board in Cranbrook and guides part-time in the summer months.

When not working as a guide for Rocky Mountain Angler in Cranbrook, Steve relaxes on one of his many favorite waters. Averaging well over 100 days on the water every year gives Steve a better understanding than almost anyone of the East Kootenay lakes. He has become well known for his willingness to teach others the art of stillwater fly fishing.

If you would like to contact Steve for a trip you may do so at 250-489-3695.

Fishing the Lakes of the Kootenays
Steve Harris

The town of Cranbrook has been my home for most of my thirty-five years. After catching my first native trout at only eight, I've been hooked ever since. The south east corner of British Columbia is known commonly as the East Kootenays. Being surrounded by the Rocky Mountains and its captivating scenery has made the outdoors my place of choice.

Lakes in the Kootenay are highly productive thanks to quality stocking programs and tighter fishing regulations. The influx of fly fishers and catch and release has helped the trout population and created better angling opportunities. There are a vast number of lakes ranging from small pothole lakes to deep clear lakes several miles long.

While winters can be quite harsh, most Kootenay lakes are ice-free by early May. After spending at least five months under thick ice the trout are ready to feed on insect life and challenge the fly fisher once again. As the water warms to above seven degrees (Celsius) the first hatches start to show. The chironomids begin their upward journey to hatch into adults to complete their cycle. The experienced fly fisher with the right pattern can catch upward of thirty fish a day when the trout are in a heavy feed. The chironomids are usually shades of black, brown and green. Some of these can reach an incredible length of one inch though most are usually about 1/4 of that size. Both floating and sinking lines are used to mimic the upward motion the chironomid makes.

As the water warms even more and the days get longer you can expect to see mayflies, damsels, dragons and even the caddis. The mayflies generally hatch in the early afternoons until dusk. Windy and overcast days are great times to experience these hatches. If there is no visible emergence of adults then nymphs below the surface should work. Best patterns to try include the Hare's Ear, Pheasant Tail or a small Halfback. When adults are present Adam's or Cahill's should produce. Hook sizes are 10 through 16. There are always those days when mayflies are hatching as well as the caddis. The adult caddis can really excite the trout and if conditions are right it can make for great dry fly fishing. The Elk Hair Caddis, Mikuluk Sedge and the Humpy work ideal. The large Travelers sedge can be matched on a size 8 hook, while the common caddis is generally about a size 14. Experiencing a caddis hatch at night fall, when large trout are slashing at the surface, is pure enjoyment.

By the month of June the days are getting warmer and longer. This triggers the migration of damsel and dragon nymphs towards the shore line. The trout key in on these large nymphs in the reed beds and cattails. When the fish are taking damsels, a sink-tip or a floating line is the ticket. Damsel imitations are tan, shades of green or even bright yellow. Size 10 to 14 long shank make nice damsels when tied slender. Jack Shaw wrote about the take on a damsel, it can be as soft as a puff of wind or as vicious as a snapping dog. This is all so true, I've missed many fish on light strikes, yet had numerous break-offs from very strong ones.

The dragonfly nymphs are a much sought after food item by trout. In late June or early July these nymphs can be seen walking the shoreline and up tall blades of grass. This is the time to hook up with a slow, full-sink line. They can be best represented with green, black or brown patterns. My first experience with the dragon nymph happened several years ago. While unloading my boat at Wapiti Lake, I noticed a large black insect climbing a nearby log. As I looked closer in the surrounding grass I found two or three more. These were migrating dragonflies and I hoped the trout had keyed in on them. In a hurry my fly rod was set up and a large nymph was tied to my tippet. To the left of the boat launch was a large stand of cattails. There seemed to be a good number of fish working that area so I rowed over and dropped anchor. I made a cast right and with two strips of the line a nice rainbow of 3 pounds intercepted my fly. The prime silver was released along with 13-14 others that afternoon. When the dragonfly nymphs are making their journey towards the shoreline, the fishing can be exceptional.

The abundance of fresh water shrimp (scuds) in our lakes is incredible. These little crustaceans are a staple for all species of trout. It's wise to have a good selection of scud patterns when heading out to the lake. Patterns such as the Baggy Shrimp in shades of green, yellow, tan and pink work best. A scud imitation fished slowly or pulled in short jerks can entice the trout into striking.

Leeches are an important food source for trout in lakes. Fishing leech patterns is by far my favorite and most productive. Because most lakes in the Kootenay have such clarity, the fish are often seen. I enjoy sight fishing with patterns tied using marabou in shades of green, brown and maroon. It's recommended to pinch the barbs on the hook because the flies are often taken back in the mouth. A certain trip I had a few years back comes to mind. A number of very large trout were surfacing on the south end of Jim Smith Lake. After trying a variety of nymphs and dry flies, I resorted to a black leech. After my third cast I connected with a rainbow just under eight pounds. A short time later I was into a second that was a solid ten pounds. The third was again a large one weighing over eight. Since that unforgettable day, I've sworn by leeches for the big trout.

By the time July and August roll around fishing may slow right down. The constant heat warms the shoal and makes it almost unbearable for the fish. The majority of them will retreat to the deeper water where the temperature is much cooler. The use of fast sinking and high-density lines are of most value. The fish will still feed on the shoal, but only at certain times of the day. Early mornings and evenings can produce well. The idea of fishing well after dark is should be tried in the Kootenays. Large patterns and the cooling of the water can produce some good results.

After summer storms or heavy winds bloodworms become dislodged from the bottom of the lake and float helplessly in the water column. Because trout don't have to exert much effort they gobble up all they wish. A bloodworm imitation on a long leader and a strike indicator rigged on a floating line often brings success. A stomach pump is useful to check the contents of fish to see what they are feeding on all year round.

The fall in the Kootenays is a beautiful time. The trees have all started turning color and the air has a certain crispness. This is the best time of the fishing season to catch big trout. With the days getting shorter and the water starting to cool down, the fish search the shallows for insect life. The return of Autumn is when the Eastern Brook trout stock up on food before their annual spawn. The sight of big brookies cruising for feed gets the adrenaline going. A well presented nymph or leech can create fantastic fall fishing. As winter approaches the brookies start to pair up with their mates, they should not be disturbed at this time.

Whether I'm fishing chironomids on a warm day in May or stripping leeches in early November the days are always enjoyable. There are many lakes to fish here and I try to visit a good number of them. With the practice of catch and release and good management of our lakes, the trout will be here for a long time to come.

Kendra Konkin

Jeff Mironuck

Jeff Mironuck has lived in the Kootenay region of B.C. for his entire life. Learning to fly fish on such waters as Kootenay Lake has allowed Jeff to become very proficient with the fly rod. Tying flies and angling keeps him busy throughout the year. Jeff's first book, Home Waters, gave him the opportunity to teach the art of fly fishing to many fellow anglers. When not guiding or teaching, Jeff enjoys everything from drifting dries on the Elk to chironomid fishing on Whiteswan.

Writing keeps him busy in the winter as he writes annually for magazines such as Fishing the West. Staying involved with Trout Unlimited and preaching catch and release is a very important part of his passion.

If you would like to contact Jeff call him at 250-489-4908 or email him at jeffmironuck@hotmail.com.

Dry Flies and the St.Mary Cutthroat
Jeff Mironuck

As the sun stretched out its fiery arms and peered over the icy Steeples I could feel the warmth graze my back and gently push me to the river bank. Early July can bring out some of my favorite river fishing and on this particular day something seemed different, almost haunting. As the hair on the back of my neck stood up I tied on an olive Elk Hair Caddis. With only 20 ft of line out and one false cast my fly graced the water. The shadows along the bank began to retreat and a large cutthroat broke surface up stream. I realized there was one less caddis on the river this morning.

* * * * * * * * * * * * * * * * * * * *

The St. Mary River begins its decent in the Purcell Mountains. Ice cold water flows down into St. Mary Lake, all the while gaining size as many smaller streams flow into the river. Meachen Creek, Redding Creek and Dewar Creek are the most notable as the themselves do hold a fair number trout. From the lake down Hellroaring Creek, Matthew Creek, Luke Creek, Perry Creek and Mark Creek join up with the river. The water found above St. Eugene's Mission is faster flowing with more small log jams and separate side channels. There are many areas open to wading and the fishing is quite good. Road access is poor but the country is hiked easily. Below the mission the river widens and with the more level ground it slows as well. Typically you will find larger fish here but the numbers will be down. As the water deepens and slows Dollies are more frequent along with suckers and squaw fish. The river continues on like this until meeting up with the Kootenay River. The St. Mary has all the makings of quality blue-ribbon stream and it should be recognized as one.

Generally you will find good numbers of cutthroat and Rocky Mountain whitefish with a few rainbows, brooks and Dolly Vardens. Unfortunately you will also find coarse fish. The cutthroat are the most sought after fish in the river by most anglers. Westslope cutthroat in general are more willing to take a fly or a spinner, they are also the most abundant fish in the river. They can be distinguished by their bright orange slashes on their throat. They are good fighting fish that take flies willingly. This is the one characteristic

100

that makes them such a good trout for learners. Throughout the river 12 inches is an average size fish with some cutthroat, rainbows and Dolly's reaching the mid 20's. Occasionally you will see a Dolly in the area of 10 to 15 pounds but often you will only be left with a broken line. Large suckers also provide some excitement for anglers. Many times I have seen experienced anglers get excited over a heavy strike only to be disappointed by a "bottom dweller". Although the are not considered a "trophy fish" by most, on the bright side they often provide some great fighting action. Fishing the bottom in slower water will allow you to hook up with these fish as well as the other larger more appealing ones.

In geological terms it is a relatively young stream. The stream bottom is formed in a "V" shape due to the steady flush of water. In spring runoff the heavy snow pack from the surrounding mountains and hills causes the tributaries and the main body of the river to gain water level, speed and also is responsible for the increased amount of debris in the water and the decreased clarity. St. Mary River is closed from April 1st until the middle of June although I would not recommend fishing it until July. The water is dirty and the currents become unpredictable and unsafe early in the season. As it flows and meanders though the drainage it constantly grows in size until reaching the lake. St. Mary Lake is incredibly important to the success and quality of the stream. It acts as a settling pond and in some cases it creates a protected haven for the habitants of the stream.

I concentrate the majority of my fishing below the lake where the river photographs into the perfect blue-ribbon, freestone trout fishery. I have drifted the river and am confident that it can be done in a safe matter throughout its length. However, I would not recommend that anyone drifts in anything less that a high quality raft or drift boat. Fishing from a raft allows the angler to cover more water and makes those hard to reach areas accessible. Be prepared to get out and lead the boat along in a few sections during periods of high water. This can easily be done by tying a sturdy rope to the stern or bow and guiding it along the rapids.

From the lake down the river is joined by several other tributaries. The most notable are Perry Creek, Hellroaring Creek, Matthew Creek and the once troubled Mark Creek. For many years Mark Creek dumped heavy pollutants into the river and made it almost completely sterile of any life below its confluence. Mark Creek flows through the small mining town of Kimberly. Until about 1979 it served the town as a convenient moving garbage disposal. Everything from road salt, dead animals and sewage to highly toxic chemicals from the mine flowed down Mark Creek into the river. Some of this is still evident in the old channels of the river today. Things such as old tires and metal drums can be found lying on the permanently yellow stained rocks. The local biologists were aware of the problems but the mine and the government were not prepared to pump out the required funds to clean up the mess. In the early 80's Kimberly and the surrounding communities began the hard work of cleaning. Today we see a pristine river and some of the best fishing and insect hatches are found below Mark Creek. In 1983 a two-fish limit was imposed and the minimum keep size was 12 inches. Unfortunately, many fishers were not informed or just did not care. The river was then changed to fly fishing only below the lake and catch and release is practiced by most anglers now. This has greatly improved the fishing and hopefully it has increased the public's awareness when it comes to protecting such a valuable resource.

As with any trout stream the St. Mary is affected by the different seasons. Winter fishing requires an angler to be dressed as a skier combined with all the necessary fishing equipment. Winter is generally known for quality nymphing. The fish are lethargic and a slowly drifted nymph will usually produce fair results. Dries and streamers require a trout to move uncomfortable distances with the exception of a streamer being passed directly in front of the fish. Strike-indicators are not allowed on the river in the fly fishing only sections. I recommend a dry line, greased at the tip so you can easily see any unfamiliar movements. Wet lines seem to do the trick when presenting streamers at all times of the year.

Spring fishing begins June 15. The water is often murky and slightly high, but the fish can still be enticed into striking. Streamer fishing is by far the most productive with the more brightly colored patterns finding a place at the end of my line. Nymphs and dries just won't work well in these messy conditions. Fish tend to hold close to the bank and feed very little. They are more concerned about protecting themselves from the onslaught of Mother Nature. Some small fish are killed off in the runoff, but as the water slows and clears the trout once again feed actively and start to move around.

Mid July starts my summer on the rivers and is a nice break from the continual lake fishing scene. About this time the lakes cool down and the water level in the river reaches that perfect point. Dry fly fishing is what the St. Mary is famous for. In the summer I can't find anything more enjoyable that drifting a hopper or an Adam's on the surface and then watching a large cutthroat either sip it under or violently attack it. Prolific hatches occur throughout the river in the summer. Caddis and mayfly are my favorites but I can't dismiss the stone flies or even the midges. Terrestrial fishing is arguably the most visual and exciting type of fly fishing on the St. Mary. July, August and September offer a good variety of crickets, grasshoppers, caterpillars and ants. The St. Mary runs through a small valley of trees, bush and grass. It's these grassy banks that breed such immense numbers of terrestrials. Hopper imitations like Dave's Hopper or Joe's Hopper work very well while almost any ant imitation will catch fish too. Near the end of August the water drops, wading becomes easy and the trout are easily brought to the surface. It's this time that I enjoy the most. A wide variety of insects are available to the fish into September and as the tourists leave for home the river is often bare of visitors.

Fall fishing can be deadly. The fish are stocking up for the long winter, everyone has left the river and the insects are few. Dries, nymph and streamers all have their days in the fall. I like to change up quite often as the trout can become very selective. The fish begin their move into the deeper water zones and they tend to become more concentrated in the larger pools. I suppose if anything streamers may be slightly more effective. Zonkers, Muddlers and Woolly Buggers tend to draw out the big fish. Nymphs also have their place. Flashbacks, stone flies and Gold Ribbed Hare's Ear nymphs should work assuming you are able to fish them deep. Warm afternoons can trigger moderate hatches of caddis and mayflies. It's best to carry all the fly boxes this time of year.

Overall it is very easy to fish the St. Mary and catch large and wild trout. This has become somewhat of a rarity over the last few years in North America. The river has been returned to its natural state and in some ways it has benefited from the pollution. It is now hard to find a summer day without experiencing some major insect hatches. The river opens it itself for the many different types and techniques fly fishing has to offer. The result is still the same, quality trout and breathtaking scenery.

Cranbrook and Kimberly provide lodging and sport shops for the fly fishers. Many prime spots on the river are within a 20 minute drive from either location. Overall the river has seen many changes through its life. A once pure stream was inundated with pollution and again cared for in only a short time. We will not know the effects man has had on this stream for quite some time. As it sits now, we are blessed with natures beauty in its natural state. Lets hope that we will have the knowledge and will to keep it this way in the future so that our following generations will be able to enjoy our fly fishing too.

* * * * * * * * * * * * * * * * * *

As my fly drifted that perfect, flawless drift a nose of a very large trout rose. I watched the trout sip in my fly and then silently eased the rod up setting the hook in the top of his mouth. As I played out my trophy it felt rewarding knowing that my creation of feathers and fur was enough to fool this seasoned cutthroat. I unhooked the large male and released him back to the stream. Returning the favor.

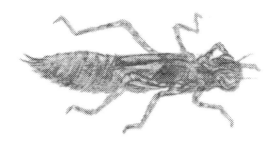

Brian Oke with a chunky cutthroat on the St. Mary

Dwayne D'Andrea of Mountain Valley Sports Fishing and Tours

The Mighty Columbia River

   With one of the most prolific hatches on any stream in B.C., the Columbia River can be a fly fishers dream river. Large pools, long runs and deep water make this a challenge to beginners but a reward to the experienced angler. With rainbows averaging 3 lbs and many between 5 and 10 lbs, the lower Columbia can attract some attention. Boats are very handy on this river but fishing from shore is possible. I strongly recommend a guided trip as these waters can be very dangerous. Some back eddies reach depths of over 100 feet and in the early season whirlpools with enough power to sink a boat can be observed.

   The Columbia River is a stream of history and memories dating back to the early 1800's. The Columbia River was a natural pathway which was followed by many travelers. Between the shores there flowed a steady stream of traffic. Natives, explorers, voyagers of the fur trade, missionaries, prospectors and eventually settlers all had their place on the mighty Columbia. The Columbia can still be viewed as it was in the early years between Castlegar and Trail. Now the main people floating the Columbia carry trout rods in search of trophy rainbows. Dry fly fishing on the Columbia is very good. Hard fighting rainbows spend much of their summer time searching the calm, clear waters for food. With countless hatches and some excellent terrestrial activity, casting dries to monster rainbows is how much of the summer fishing is done. Hoppers are very popular among the local fly fishers. Bait and lure fishers also enjoy this river and some spots can get crowded on the weekends.

   Sturgeon fishing is available on a catch and release basis with this being one of the best spots in B.C. to still angle for them. Guided trips are necessary if you plan to try and land one of the Columbia River sturgeon.

   Fishing on the Columbia is best from May through October. In the early season large black and golden stones fill up the trout after the long cold winter. Nymph fishing can be fantastic at this time of the year. Stimulators and Sofa Pillows imitate the dry a little later on. Always carry grass hopper and ant patterns through out the season. It's possible to fish hoppers from June until October with other hatches such as mayflies, stone flies and the thick caddis hatches in between. Many anglers travel from all over to fish this stream and the size and quantity of the rainbow make it very comparable to

An Elk River tributary - Photo by David Lambroughton

Elk River cutthroat - Photo by John Geirach

the Bow River in Alberta.

Bald eagles, White tail deer, Geese, Blue Herring and bears can all be seen on the Columbia. The entire area of the Kootenays has not yet been hit with the wave of commercialism that can so often be seen on other areas equal in fishing opportunities. Much of the Columbia River Basin is preserved in its pristine wilderness state.

There are many places that offer great accommodations in Castlegar and Trail. Restaurants are numerous with everything from Chinese food to home cooked meals on the river banks. Camping is available at Syringa Creek Provincial Park and Kootenay River Park.

If you do get a chance to get over to the Columbia, be sure to look up Dwayne D'Andrea of Mountain Valley Sports Fishing and Tours. He is a wealth of knowledge on the area and his experience has left him a great guide. He can be reached at 1-800-554-5684 or 250-365-5771.

David Brown

Growing up in Hamilton Ontario, David Brown was introduced to the sport of fly fishing at 15 years old. During those early beginnings David cut his teeth on small mouth bass, native brook trout and Great Lakes steelhead. He moved to Calgary Alberta in 1987, where he has resided ever since.

David discovered the Elk River while on a fishing trip 7 years ago, upon realizing the potential, he began guiding on the Elk the following season, by doing so he established the first fly fishing only guide service in the area. David's guide service's The Elk River Angler and the sister company, The Alberta River Angler now spend the summer and fall months guiding their client's on the trout waters of south eastern B.C. and south western Alberta. With the strong fly fishing background that David has, and the experienced guides he employs it's easy to see why he and his companies have established themselves as the premier guide services in their respective areas. To add to his credentials, David has been certified by the Federation of Fly Fishermen as a fly casting instructor.

Prior to relocating to Fernie B.C. for the guiding season, David spends his time fishing and guiding on the Bow River. Along with his keen interest in fly fishing David's other main interests are his wife Leah and his 17 month old daughter Hope. David can be reached in Calgary at 403-248-6612 From July 1st to Sept 30th he is in Fernie. 250-423-9231 (days) 250-423-3654 (evenings).

Dry Flies and the Elk River
David Brown

As the furthest east river n B.C., the Elk River begins at Elk Lakes and charts its 110 mile course south west as it makes its way to lake Koocanusa. During its voyage it cuts its way through some of the most spectacular terrain in the Rockies, gathering fertile tributaries as it goes. The river passes under mountains with names like Ghostrider, Three Sisters and Hosmer. Fernie and its valley are home to moose, deer, elk, Rocky Mountain sheep, goats, cougars and bears. It's easy to see why this valley was the favorite hunting ground for the Kootenay Indians.

The Elk River is a river of varied character, in its beginning it is a meandering meadow stream, and in its end it is a raging torrent that slices its way through a hodo rimmed canyon. Like the river, the valley's character and vegetation also change as it descends down through the Rocky Mountain trench. Forests along the middle river could easily be mistaken for a Pacific Coastal rain forest, complete with huge cedar trees. Out in the "South Country" at rivers end reminds me of the countryside along Montana's Missouri river, less the rattle snakes. White settlers came to the valley in the late 19th century mainly to mine the rich seams of coal that are still being mined today. Towns that line the valley owe their existence to the mines which is the Elk Valley's largest employer. The railway line that parallels the river has some of the longest trains in North America, their 1OO+ hopper cars laden with coal are destined for worldwide consumption via the port of Vancouver. Along with the spectacular scenery, over the years what has drawn myself to the Elk River has been the excellent cutthroat trout fishing the river has to offer.

The Elk River Season and Hatches

The season on the Elk River legally begins June 15th and ends April 1st. Opening day can find the river high with runoff. Generally it is fishable by early July. This is a great time of year to be on the River, as it is Golden Stone fly time. These big bugs really get the fish looking up and nymph fishing can be spectacular. This is a great time to break out your big dry fly attractor patterns such as Stimulators our Turk's Tarantulas, don't be afraid to give the fly a little action as the cutthroats tend to key in on insects that appear to be getting away from them. Any stone fly nymph pattern works well on the Elk River, over the years my favorite has been the Charlie

Brooks Montana Stone. A close second would be Anderson's Rubber Leg Stone. Pattern sizes should be #6 - #10 for both dries and nymphs. This great hatch will last for most of July and sometimes into early August. The early season also sees caddis flies appearing on the scene. They last all summer and into the fall ending with the bruiser of the caddis family, the October caddis. Imitations such as the Elk Hair Caddis or small Stimulators work well for the adult, for pupae I recommend David Lambroughton's Flash Back caddis. All caddis patterns should range in size from 8 for the October caddis down to 16 for the smaller sedges. Mayfly hatches add to the early season feeding frenzy, Green Drakes appear first, Royal Wulffs or H+L variants usually do the deed but if the fish get selective extended body patterns do the trick. A good nymph pattern for this bug is a Flashback Bead Head Pheasant Tail or a Gold Ribbed Hare's Ear nymph.

As the river drops in late July watch for P.M.D.'s and yellow and lime Sallies. Ausable Wulffs and the Parachute Adams are my favorite imitations for the P.M.D.'s. For the small stone flies use yellow and lime Trudes or small Stimulators. All these bugs will hatch into August. Midges are also an important food source for Elk River cutthroats. These little bugs hatch all season long and can provide some challenging small dry fly fishing. #18 - #20 Parachute Adams or Griffith Gnats are the flies of choice for this hatch, watch likely looking dry fly spots in the early morning or evening.

August on the Elk River sees the arrival of the terrestrials, namely hoppers and flying ants. Both of these land based bugs end up being trout food upon their arrival to the water. Searching the water with a favorite hopper pattern results in aggressive takes while the arrival of the flying ants means sipping rises. Ant patterns should be in smaller sizes and hopper patterns should be carried in a good variety. Late summer sees the end of the P.M.D.'s and the arrival three new players that will last into the fall.

October caddis make their appearance in late August. This large insect draws fish up out of the holes as they skitter across the surface laying eggs. The best imitation for this sedge is a Orange or Royal Stimulator. Joining the October caddis is the infamous Blue Winged Olive and when conditions are right these two can create a feeding frenzy. Break out the small Parachute Adams or Comparaduns for this one!

The Elk River also gets a hatch of Red Quills, this handsome mayfly can be imitated by a Parachute Adams or an Ausable Wulff in sizes 14-16. Like all trout streams, fishing to rising fish usually means locating feeding fish in low light or on overcast days. The Elk River is no exception. The main difference with the Elk is that it's not as fertile as many other rivers, therefore hatches can be sparse at times. The good news is that cutthroats by nature will eat anything that floats by. While on the river with author John Gierach, we caught a cutthroat that had what looked like a lure of some sort was stuck in its mouth. On closer examination we realized it was a mouse! All though trout feeding on mice is quite common, keep in mind this fish was only ten inches long.

When fishing the Elk or any river for that matter, it helps to know what hatches are in progress. On the Elk for example, if it is October caddis time, but you are not seeing any on the water you would not be wrong fishing a imitation such as a Stimulator to likely holding water from the boat or while wading.

A nice cutthroat caught in a tributary of the Elk

Fishing and Floating the Elk River

The Elk River is a very user friendly river. There is good access all the way along its course. The upper section from the Elk Lakes down to Line Creek is easy walk and wade water, the stretch from Line Creek to Elko is best suited to floating and the canyon stretch down to the mouth can be tackled by rafting if you know what you are doing. I spend most of my time on the floatable stretches above Elko, and for first timers to the river the stretch from Hosmer to Fernie is a good days float.

The drill for this river is to fish dry flies or streamers from the boat, then stop and work the holding water then move on to the next spot. For the wading angler it's very much the same except you are on foot as opposed to being in a boat. Success on this river means working various types of holding water, everything from boulder gardens to log jams can be found on this river, and more times then not they harbor cutthroat trout. Large holes are worth trying out. Streamer patterns and sink tip line can be very effective. The long slow pools are the domain of the bull trout, or Dolly Varden as it is called locally. They can grow up to 20lbs.

Nymphing on the Elk means heavily weighted bead heads and yarn indicators, very little external weight is needed for this river and nymphing can produce some very good results as far as numbers of fish are concerned. Although the Elk River is easy to float, it can also turn into a dangerous river if you are not cautious, the river has eaten a drift boat from time to time so watch for sweepers and as a rule of thumb stick to the main channel as much as possible.

Equipment

If I had to choose one rod for the Elk River it would be a 9ft 5wt. This rod can do anything required on this river, but owning one rod is not as much fun and is perhaps the reason I get ugly looks from my better half as I try to justify my latest addition to the arsenal. For dry flies out of the boat I would use a 2-5 wt. 7 1/2-9ft long. For throwing big attractor patterns from the boat a 9ft, 4-6wt handles the job quite nicely. As for chasing bull trout I like to use a #5 or #6 nine feet in length. Weight forward floating lines for all these rods is all you need, however if you are serious about chasing bull trout bring a 10 ft. sink tip just in case. Clothing for this part of the world is important, rain gear is a must, along with a good pullover fleece for when the sun starts to drop.

In the summer months it is possible to wade wet, however do bring along waders for those chilly days. Polarized sunglasses, sunscreen and a hat are also necessary, don't forget your tour camera and film.

Anglers looking for a place to camp should check out Fernie Provincial park. If you are seeking motels, B&B's etc. I recommend calling Fernie Reservations at 1-888-754-7325 or Country Roads at 1-250-423-7905. Rip & Richards located in Fernie on Hwy #3 at the south end of town is a good bet for a great meal and a cold one after a day on the river.

British Columbia's Region 6

River country. The Skeena is a very large region, bordered by Alaska and the Yukon on the north and Tweedsmuir Park on the south. In my opinion the most noted trout waters in the province can all be found here in region 6. The Bulkley, Morice, Babine and Kispiox are just a few of them. Great steelhead fishing coupled with unforgettable trout fishing make a trip to this region the trip of a lifetime. For those fortunate enough to fish here regularly, the thought of world record salmon and steelhead has to make you question ever fishing elsewhere. Smaller waters such as the Kitimat and Kitlope should not be overlooked. Many guides operate in this region and it's recommended you get one if unfamiliar with the waters. Lodges and camps operate on most rivers and with 26 classified waters it's the heaviest classified region in the province.

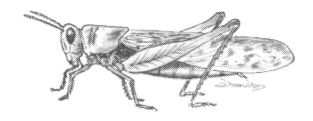

Pierce Clegg

Pierce Clegg owner and operator of Babine Norlakes Lodge since 1986. Pierce offers everyone from novice to experienced anglers a chance to enjoy the beautiful mountain scenery and world class rainbows and steelhead. Ultimate dry fly fishing is found on the Babine. It's rated as one of the best rainbow fisheries in B.C. The charming history of the lodge and cabins will give you a special feeling of warmth and relaxation. When Pierce gets a chance he enjoys chasing trophy rainbows in his backyard and spending time with his family. Pierce spear headed the Babine Watershed Land Resource Use Plan for the Babine which resulted in the Babine River Corridor becoming a class A provincial park.

The Babine Norlakes Lodge is famous for offering the fly fishing experience of a life time. Pierce can be contacted at 250-847-6160 or fax him at 250-847-3444.

117

Rainbows and Steelhead of the Babine
Pierce Clegg

Any place on earth where there is a huge lake with a gentle outflow, and a connection to the ocean that allows anadromous fish to migrate into it's headwaters, there you will find incredible fish and wildlife values.

Babine Lake, 110 miles long, the largest natural freshwater lake in B.C., and the Babine River, a soon to be Class A Provincial Park, is such a place where many a fishery biologist has studied, written about, and marveled in it's unique habitat qualities. Before the first pioneer efforts of the Hudson Bay Company, First Nation people were the only ones living and benefiting from the rich fishery and wildlife of the Babine watershed. Although logging and mining have changed some of the qualities of the Babine watershed, she is still largely intact as a semi to full wilderness area. Visitors are still astounded at the richness and beauty of the place, and tourism lodges like Babine Norlakes Lodge, in business since 1950, have built a reputation upon the wild stocks of trout and steelhead of the Babine.

The lake, it's tributaries, and it's outflow river section of about twelve miles is a prime and rich nursery for it's fishery of rainbow trout, cutthroat trout, lake trout, burbot, bull trout, steelhead and four Pacific salmon types; sockeye, pink, coho and chinook. There are whitefish, suckers and a variety of coarse fish not fully understood nor appreciated. Like many fisheries, there are obvious events and many mysteries perhaps never to be fully understood. I have been angling guiding there since 1986. My mind is now losing track of the many unbelievable stories that can come from such a world class fishery! I will try in the following paragraphs to give the reader a feel for a fishing season on the river beginning in May and ending in November.

In the far north, the advent of the spring "break up" is a long overdue experience. Northern winters are long and dark with daylight hours reduced as the earth shifts it's axis. People get squirrelly, especially the anglers who can't wait to wet a line again. The entire Babine Lake has been frozen over so thick that logging trucks could drive on it! The southern end of the lake breaks up first, and the northern end where the Babine river begins, is the last section to break up. This occurs in early May on average. Break up may occur in April or late May depending on the weather. I have witnessed break up from April 27th to May 18th. If your a fish in the winter, you too are looking forward to spring break up because you will receive your first great meal of the season, salmon fry. Two sockeye spawning enhancement channels on the Fulton River and Pinkut Creek (tributaries to the Babine Lake) plus the wild stock salmon spawning areas almost guarantee that hundreds of millions on salmon fry will hatch in May to early June. All spawning tributaries on Babine Lake become feeding frenzy areas for all fish living in the lake. But perhaps the most famous of all events takes place on the very upper end of the Babine River near Fort Babine. That famous area has been named "Rainbow Alley." Picture this salmon fry hatch and migration through the funnel of Rainbow Alley. It's like Custard's Last Stand, no word of a lie, only the fry outnumber the trout feeding on them, but the number of trout in that relatively small area is astounding. This slaughter of fry and gorging of trout goes on for about a month, from mid May to mid June, then a different food source for the trout takes over for most of the summer. Golden stone flies and mayflies with some caddis, weather and water conditions permitting, provide the next great meal for trout. The upper end of the Babine River, specifically the Fly Fishing Only Section of the Babine River, includes a 7 mile long lake called Nilkitkwa Lake. The shallow shoals, islands, channels and drop-offs plus great weed beds make up one of our globes finest salmon and trout nurseries. Nilkitkwa Lake is a classic example and study for any serious angler or biologist, not to mention a great place for trout to live, eat and grow. The mayflies rule in Nilkitkwa Lake feeding both the spring hatched salmon fry and the trout we love to hunt. This lake is also home to some of the biggest trout ever landed in the Babine watershed.

The Fly Fishing Only Section of the Babine River extends from Fort Babine to one kilometer below the Federal Fisheries Weir on the Babine River, a twelve mile section in all. Nilkitkwa Lake is basically in the middle of the fly only section. It too is fly only thank God. The outlet of Nilkitkwa Lake to the weir and a little bit below the weir is home to some of the most incredible Golden stone fly hatch angling anywhere in the world. This section is relatively small, say one mile in length, but highly concentrated in fish and bugs. This feeding frenzy is much like the spring salmon fry event, and they both have a great angling love in common; both are dry line, on the surface action, target casting to rainbows up to ten pounds.

This is not a hatchery fishery, or fish planted fishery. All trout in the Babine watershed are wild, diverse and strong fighters.

Late summer brings a slow down in insect hatches and a slow down in trout concentration where anglers easily notice them. They are still around, but harder to find and catch. There are exceptions to this, and I cannot predict the where, when, why and how enough to talk about that now. There is one major change to the fishery occurring at this time; the arrival of the salmon run. This starts about mid July, but really gets going mid August to mid September. The food chain in fish and wildlife that surrounds this annual pilgrimage of salmon is nothing short of spiritual. The amount of eggs and carcass laid down by the salmon is a sight only one can fully appreciate by being here to see it. The salmon spawn and die, the fish eat their eggs and flesh, the small and large game, especially bear, gorge on the flesh whether fresh or rotten, the birds and waterfowl also indulge, and I have seen many living things that I thought were not a part of this food chain partake in the annual banquet.

The steelhead are a different breed than the salmon although steelhead are biologically classified as a salmon. Steelhead migrate from the ocean to spawn in the Babine watershed too, but they take much longer to consider their destiny, waiting to spawn in the spring although they arrive very early for that event. The steelhead also eat eggs and perhaps eat salmon carcass as well. Perhaps this is why they follow the salmon, just for the food that will sustain them. And, the steelhead do not all die after spawning. Somewhere around ten to twenty percent return to the ocean to someday return again to spawn. Some steelhead even return a second, third and even fourth time! This is truly an amazing fish with an amazing journey. In the spring time, when steelhead are spawning, and when some are thinking about returning to the ocean again, the salmon smolt are migrating to the ocean from the lake and river watershed. These two year old juvenile salmon are about five inches long, millions of them, and they are another great meal for fish. So when some steelhead decide to return to the ocean after spawning, they have smolt to eat on the way! Mother nature is indeed timely and balanced beyond our comprehension or appreciation.

I fish steelhead from late August to mid November, weather permitting on the November side of things. The Babine steelhead are second to none in size, beauty and power. World records have come and gone with no advertisement. Those secrets are best left untold. Perhaps the Babine steelhead magic can best be summed up by saying that the spirit of the river speaks to those who are lucky enough to know her. She is not invincible to the development plans of logging, etc., and her days are numbered like so many great watersheds. But, for now, she is there functioning as best she can given the state of our world environment. Another attribute of her world class steelhead waters is the number and concentration of classic holding water runs and pools. That together with a gentle gradient backed up by the huge consistency of water flows from Babine Lake make this river un-comparable.

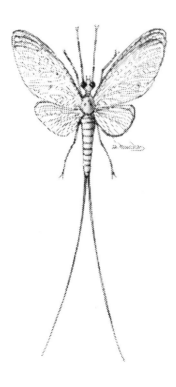

Feeling lonely on the Kitlope River

The Scenic Kitlope River
Ed Wilson

The Kitlope River and its tributaries form a watershed that is the largest totally intact temperate zone rain forest ecosystem on earth. Its estuary, 120 kms from Kitimat, lies at the head of the Gardener Canal-an offshoot of the Douglas Channel in north west British Columbia. The area is remarkable for its pristine beauty and its status as an ecological paradise. Indeed the Kitlope has recently been added to the B.C. Parks system. Adding in Tweedsmuir Park to its east and Fiordland to its west the whole area becomes an immense ecosystem preserve.

Unlike its largest neighboring rivers the Skeena to the north and the Dean to the south, the Kitlope has very poor steelhead and salmon runs. In the third and fourth week of July the Kitlope has the largest run of sockeye on the north central coast of B.C. Pink and chum salmon run from the last week of July to the end of August. Coho salmon run from mid August to the end of September. There are a few trout, Dolly Varden are small but plentiful. Whereas the Kitlope does not match some other rivers in angling potential it is the loneliest of places, a retreat for naturalists and lovers of the wilderness. If you wish to enjoy the Kitlope and have some great fishing at the same time, I suggest the third and fourth weeks of August. The weather is generally good and the chance of catching coho, pinks and chum at the same time is very good. Furthermore the runoff is past by this time giving rise to optimal conditions for fly fishing for these three species of salmon. Using the same equipment for the Kitlope salmon as any other salmon stream in B.C. will be adequate.

Access to the Kitlope is difficult by reason of distance, the absence of any roads, the few places to set down aircraft and the inability to negotiate the river without a jet boat. There are no air strips. You may be able to land a float plane on the very wide lower Kitlope and on Kitlope Lake there is enough room to land a helicopter on a few of the beaches. This is definitely the sort of place where a fully equipped guide would be useful.

There are no accommodations or permanent structures on the Kitlope and none are allowed. There are some locations where you may camp in a tent temporarily. The park is designed to be maintained in its pristine state and operated on the "whatever you take in you take out" principle.

Kitimat City with its nearby airport at the head of the Douglas Channel is the natural departure point for a trip to the Kitlope. Kitimat has all the perquisites for the holidaying angler. While in the city try a few casts in the Kitimat River. The Kitimat is also very scenic and some consider it the most productive stream in the Douglas Channel.

For a guided trip to the Kitlope, contact Pat Wilson of Alta-B.C. Tours at 403-288-1769. You may also send him a fax at 403-288-1768. Colin Light at Cuttys Fly and Tackle can be reached at 1-888-2CUTTYS or 250-632-5655. He can provide you with some up to date information and get you outfitted for an excellent wilderness adventure.

South Western Alberta

Fly fishing in southern Alberta offers the angler countless lakes and streams where it can be done almost all year for trophy fish. Although the area is not known for its quality lakes, there are still many that can be very comparable to some of B.C.'s best. Lake fishing in the higher areas of Alberta can be fantastic. Most lakes are stalked regularly with trout and pressure on many lakes is minimal. These trout tend to take whatever is presented to them and this gives anglers of all skill levels the opportunity for a great day of fishing. The lower level lakes can hold many species of fish other than trout. Pike and walleye fishing is very popular with many anglers. Lakes in Alberta are often over shadowed by British Columbia's famous waters, however, when one speaks of rivers in south western Canada, the great trout rivers of Alberta can steal all the attention. Trophy rivers like the Bow and Crowsnest draw anglers from all over the world. In the next few chapters some of the most experienced anglers will guide you to some of their favorites. Stew Slymon offers his expert opinion on lake fishing in southern Alberta while other focus on the blue ribbon waters. Enjoy their knowledge and then plan a trip for yourself.

Stew Slymon

Stew Slymon currently resides in Okotoks, Alberta and works in the Oil and Gas Industry. Stew has been fly fishing for over thirty years all over North America and has given fly fishing seminars both in Alberta and B.C. on fly fishing stillwaters. Honing his lake fishing skills in the best stillwater fishing on the planet, the B.C. interior, Stew has taken this experience and adapted them to the lakes of Southern Alberta. Pursuing other passions like mountaineering and skiing, Stew manages 60 to 70 days in a rather short angling season chasing large fish where ever he can find them.

FLY FISHING THE LAKES OF
SOUTHERN ALBERTA
Stew Slymon

Southern Alberta has lakes? That certainly could be the response given by visiting anglers or even resident anglers for that matter. When you have world class fisheries such as the Bow and the Crowsnest Rivers at your doorstep, it's hard for many anglers to think of southern Alberta in terms of stillwater fly fishing. Believe me, it is there, it is alive, and for the most part, doing well. The fact that this part of the province is known for its Blue Ribbon stream fisheries is why I like to encourage all anglers to experience the wealth of stillwater fly fishing potential that southern Alberta has to offer. As word of the Bow and Crowsnest spread, the number of anglers has increased dramatically, and this increased pressure has had its impact on both these fisheries. So for those visiting anglers, or even the local who wants something a little different or simply wants to get away from the maddening crowds, please read on.

To suggest that southern Alberta has a wealth of stillwater fly fishing potential is not far from the truth. From the alpine gemstones of the east slope of the Rockies to the sloughs and impoundments of the prairies, these lakes offer the angler a variety of fish species as well as environments in which to fish. The lakes I describe in this short piece are by no means meant to be a definitive list. They are simply a few of my favorites. All anglers should be aware that many lakes, especially Alberta lakes, are prone to seasonal fish kills. If there is any doubt, check before wasting a lot of time fishing a body of water devoid of fish!! This and other useful information is usually available through local fly shops or the nearest Provincial Fish and Wildlife office. The Alberta Fishing Regulations offer a list of these offices as well as listing current closures and restrictions. Please read these carefully before setting out to any of these lakes. I have avoided listing lakes in National Parks as these are covered by other publications. I would also like to implore that those who fish these waters do so with a great deal of respect for both their inhabitants and the environments within whose boundaries they exist but above all enjoy! They are special.

Alpine lakes are wonderful places. For over thirty years I have explored the Rockies pursuing another passion, mountaineering. I would pass by these gems and wonder what secrets they held and would promise myself to return with a fly rod in hand instead of an ice axe. One shouldn't fish these lakes with large fish in mind. Rarely do these waters produce the richer aquatic environments necessary to grow large fish. Altitude and a narrow window of opportunity between ice-off and freeze-up are major factors. Insects and certain invertebrates that are the predominant food sources for these fish require rich, healthy and abundant weed beds and plenty of light to promote this growth. Because of this relative shortage of food the fish are more often opportunistic feeders than their foothill cousins and are usually not shy about taking a reasonably presented fly. I encourage the use of barb-less hooks and feel that if you don't practice catch and release all of the time, these lakes should be the exception. After all, it's not the size of the fish that inhabit these lakes that draw us to them, it is the majesty of their location. Depending on altitude, ice-off can be as late as July and freeze-up as early as September. Many of these lakes require an effort to get there and this for me is another part of the overall satisfaction in fishing alpine lakes. Fish take on a special aura when you have to work for them.

Anglers should be aware that the alpine environment can be a harsh one. I have experienced nasty snowstorms in August as well as intense sunlight and heat all on the same day. Besides carrying fishing gear, the proper clothing, first aid kit and emergency equipment should be mandatory. You should also be aware that you are in bear country and the necessary actions should be taken to avoid direct contact with them. You are invading their home turf so respect that fact. This alone should give the angler a good reason to practice catch and release. A dead fish in a pack or creel can very easily attract a hungry bruin. As for gear, I normally fish alpine lakes with a 4 weight system. Again the fish are usually not that large and the flies used to catch them are also small making the 4 weight an ideal choice. This is the kind of fishing that pack rods were invented for and can be a major plus. The advent of super light float tubes and wading equipment has revolutionized alpine lake fishing. A lot of these lakes cannot be fished very well from the shoreline. Packing in this equipment can make a big difference to the success of your trip. Line choice can be a little tricky. I like a floating line for top fishing as well as fishing chironomid pupae below surface and an intermediate sinking line and 10 Ft. sink tip for those special conditions. As far as fly selection goes, I usually think small for those lakes above tree line and a little larger for those below. For those above tree line I make sure my fly box has plenty of chironomid pupae patterns in sizes 14, 16 and 18 and scuds from size 10 to 18. Mayfly nymphs and adult patterns (usually Callibaetis), in sizes 14 to 8 can work well too. Throw in some small ants and boatmen patterns and you are set. Lakes at or below the tree line are usually more bio-diverse so you should carry and assortment of the above as well as damsel, dragonfly and leech patterns in various sizes and shades. I prefer leader lengths of 12 to 20 ft. depending on the conditions.

The lakes of the foothills are for the most part trout lakes like their alpine cousins. The major difference between the alpine and foothills lakes lies in the greater biodiversity of the foothill lakes. The lower elevation of foothill water allows for a longer ice-off period and this means more food and more feeding opportunities for

A monster pike taken on the fly rod by Stew Slymon

the fish. The result, of course, means larger fish for the angler. Hatches on these lakes are usually more frequent and heavier so the angler should be prepared with an overall selection of lake patterns. Rods in the 4 to 6 wt. class are norm for these lakes. I like to carry two or three rods, one a 4 wt. for surface presentations and 6 wt. for sub surface work. These lakes would be similar to lakes of the B.C. interior and those anglers who are knowledgeable with the methods and techniques to take fish there will feel right at home on these waters.

To the uninitiated, the prairies of southern Alberta would seem a rather barren environment, devoid of anything that would be of interest to fly fishermen, but I urge you to look further. Not only are there literally hundreds of lakes and reservoirs of all sizes, they are stocked with a large variety of species that offer the angler plenty of fun opportunities. Yes there are few decent trout lakes but that is not what brings me to these flatland shores, it is the trophy pike. Yes, Pike! It is now becoming well known that pike will take a properly presented and properly sized fly with a ferocity that can only be experienced. In fact, not only can you catch large pike subsurface with flies, but they will, under the right conditions, give the angler some superb top-water fishing that simply should not be missed. Generally speaking the best producing waters for large pike are large themselves. I find that to cover these large bodies of water properly, a small boat and motor can be a major plus to the success of your day. Trying to tube long distances all day long can spoil your outing, especially if you are battling a strong prairie wind. Speaking of wind, no one should consider fishing these large lakes without serious consideration to the fly fishermen's worst enemy. Not only can the wind make fishing difficult on the prairies, it can be a matter of life and death. These large lakes are quite shallow and when the wind blows in hard, you simply must get off the water if you are in anything but the largest of boats. Be prepared, and assume you will have to deal with wind at some point during the day. Another bonus to fishing prairie lakes is the proliferation of bird life. I am always amazed at the variety and have spent many an idle moment watching pelicans and other exotic birds swimming by. Although it is the pike that are the main draw, there are other fish here that one should not ignore. Large whitefish and perch can be caught on standard trout gear and provide some great top action on a 4 wt. system between rounds with large pike. The gear for pike on the other hand, is substantially different and lightweight trout gear will simply be destroyed by a large, aggressive fish. My choice has been a long (10 ft.), very stiff 9wt. rod that not only can toss the large flies required but the additional length will give you better leverage when fighting these very long, heavy fish. A solid line covers ninety percent of most situations. The leaders are also of major importance. Commercial pike leaders are available and if you are not comfortable with tying your own, then pay out the bucks and buy one. I prefer to tie my own and normally use a very stiff, abrasion-resistant mono. The leaders are normally quite short, 6 ft. being standard. I simply attach a 15 to 20 pound test, three foot length of mono to the fly line and then to that I tie in a 50 pound "shock tippet", also three feet long. Always check your shock tippet after each fish. Pike have very large teeth that can shred mono quite easily. The flies are generally large and I like to use 3/0 tarpon style hooks that have the barb pinched back. As far as presentation goes, I prefer to anchor and cast rather than just troll the fly. It is a lot more fun and usually far more productive. Fish over 45 inches (115 cm) are considered trophy fish.

Dave Campbell

Dave Campbell owns and operates South Bow Anglers Ltd. Dave has fished the Bow since 1979 and has guided the Bow and Southern Alberta since 1985. Dave is also a founding member and first President of the Fly Fishing Outfitters Association of Alberta. Dave's wife Barb McDonald is also in the fishing business as owner of South Bow Shuttles. They can be reached at (403) 271-7756, or email them. southbow@cadvision.com.

The Mighty Bow River
Dave Campbell

Wow! That's the biggest trout I've ever caught! If I had a dollar or doughnut for every time I've heard this, in my time as a Bow River guide, I'd either have enough money to buy a fancy new fly rod or be too fat to stand.

The Bow has, rightfully, gained a reputation for very large shouldered, hard fighting brown and rainbow trout. Browns less than 24" won't get much attention at the tackle shop, and the same can be said of rainbows shy of 22". You can expect these bruisers to be in the 3-6 pound range. Also being home to these larger fish, are numerous fish in the 10" to 18" range to satisfy any angler. The key to successfully fishing, the Bow, in one word is "diversity". Many are the days you will "pitch" streamers in the morning, dredge deep nymphs in the afternoon, and cast small dry flies at night. If the flies or methods you are employing are not working you must be willing to adapt, your rig, accordingly to find out what is. The mood of Bow river fish can change from day to day or from hour to hour.

The Bow originates at the glacially fed Bow Lake high in Alberta's' Rocky Mountains (elevation 6300 feet) and travels a tumultuous path through a wide mountain valley marked by large tracts of fir, pine, and spruce forest, to its confluence with the Kananaskis river, upstream from the town of Canmore. The most productive section of the river is between Canmore and the Arrowood bridge. There are a handful of outfitters who work the "upper" river (Canmore) and the "lower" river (below Carsland) but the designated "trophy" stretch begins in Calgary's Fish Creek Park and meanders through a lush prairie valley some 55 kilometers to the Carseland Weir. The valley is home to countless numbers of birds (herons, hawks, eagles, ducks, and geese) along with many mule deer, and a multitude of coyotes to serenade you while you fish the evening caddis hatch.

Although portions of the river remain open all year, fishing is most predictable from May through early October. A 1-2 week hiatus is necessary in June due to annual spring mountain run off. If you plan to fish the river in June please go armed with some local knowledge and alternate fishing plans. The Bow can turn to pea soup in a matter of hours.

Pre runoff fishing is best done with deep nymph rigs. San Juan worms, Prince nymphs, and Golden stone flies, being the flies of choice. Dry fly fishing can be a little spotty, but the predominant hatches are midges, Blue Winged Olives, and if you are lucky, March Brown mayflies. These large bugs (size 12-14) can sometimes be the only thing that will get the fish "on top" before the emergence of their favorite bug, the caddis fly.

Post runoff fishing begins, normally, the last week of June but times can vary, depending on snow pack and weather conditions. The water at this time will be high, off color, and lapping at or over the banks, creating back channels that in October will be virtually dry. These "rivers", with names like Guide Maker, and G-Run, hold good numbers of fish and should be angled as any small stream. Main river fishing is most productive when visibility reaches 18" or more. This is chuck and duck fishing at its finest. The object of the game is to pitch heavily weighted streamers (Clousers, Bow River Buggers, and Girdle Buggers) as close to the bank as possible, and not be killed, by one of those missiles, hurtling past your ear, in the process. The angler who can keep his fly within a foot of the bank is usually quite successful. A sinking tip fly line can help keep your fly in the strike zone longer. Some of the largest browns of the year succumb to this technique. During this time, Pale Morning duns appear, look for them in backwater channels and oxbow areas. Fish are more likely to rise in these areas due to the heavy, stained water of the main river. Also, look for Golden stone flies now, (there numbers have grown steadily in recent years) emergence can be sporadic, but spectacular if it is timed properly.

By the first week of July the water begins to drop and clear and the caddis fly makes its first appearance. Light nymphing the banks with yarn indicators and Hare's Ear and Pheasant Tail bead head nymphs can be a deadly combination with dry fly caddis fishing in the late afternoon and evening. Bow river fish are just wild about their caddis flies, and understandably so, these bugs hatch in dizzying numbers until mid October.

If you want to enjoy the dry fly caddis fishing, at it's best, be prepared to fish at dusk and beyond. Emerging and egg laying caddis will be on the water, and the discernible angler, with heron-like attentiveness, will be looking for rising fish. We call this, searching for "snouts", All you see is the snout of the fish penetrating the surface film as he searches out his dinner. Fish loose a little discretion, at this time, due to the large number of selections on the menu, and the fading light. Look for them in very thin water, sometimes exposing their dorsal fin.

Fly patterns are not much of a concern. Elk Hair caddis, in sizes 14-18, still account for many fish. If they turn finicky try a Goddard, Yarn Wing, or CDC caddis in the appropriate size and color.

By the second week of August thoughts turn to terrestrial fishing. In dry years, great numbers of grasshoppers call the cliffs and grassy banks of the Bow, home. On blustery summer afternoons a sufficient number of them are blown into the river and fish take great delight in "sipping" them down. I say "sipping" because unlike many other rivers, the largest, Bow River fish only dimples the water as it sucks down a size 8 hopper. I've had many clients say "my hopper just disappeared" before realizing it had really been "eaten".

The most common approach to hopper fishing is a technique called the "Hopper/Dropper". First secure a 5-7 ft. 2X leader to a high floating hopper (Gords, Stimulator) and then, from the bend of the hook attach a 2-4 ft piece of 3X-4X tippet, then tie on a bead head nymph. The hopper will act as a strike indicator for the nymph. Once again, Hare's Ear, Pheasant Tail and caddis pupa and larva patterns are popular choices in sizes 12-16. This style of fishing can be employed until late September.

Trico fishing from mid August until early September can be quite a challenge. Small flies, skinny water with large wary fish await the dedicated anglers who pursue this hatch. Try trico parachutes or spent wings in sizes 18-22. At this time, it is often quite effective to fish an ant or beetle during the hatch or to any other fish you see rising throughout the day.

By mid September the Blue Wing Olives begin to appear again. These bugs just love foul weather. The heaviest hatch I've witnessed was on a 5C day with heavy sleet. The entire Bow had a blue, gray tinge to it. This hatch is for the hardy, but great rewards await. An Adam's is hard to beat in sizes 18-22. Also, it's best to have some CDC or Comparaduns on hand. By early October most of the insects have stopped hatching for the year but deep nymphing the pools with San Juan Worms can be quite effective. The fish know winter is coming and its time to "beef up". Make sure your rig is getting hung up on the bottom occasionally or you're not fishing deep enough.

One thing I would like to point out to visiting anglers is the deadly threat that Whirling disease posses to Alberta's waters. Please ensure all fishing tackle (rods, reels, lines, boats, waders) are thoroughly sterilized before fishing our waters. Otherwise, come and enjoy all the Bow has to offer and maybe you will be fortunate enough to say "that's the largest trout I've every caught."

Dave Campbell has outlined 3 of the best floats on the Bow River. Being such a popular river and one with great size for the angler new to the area these should get you started in the right direction. It is highly recommended that you take a guide if new to these waters. The Bow can create a good challenge to even the best anglers.

1. Glenmore Trail - Policeman's Flats (18km/11miles). This section begins in the city of Calgary and winds its way southeast through Fish Creek park where it exits suburbia. This section features the attraction of big brown trout that are too fat, and lazy to travel far from the best spawning beds in town. A pleasant 5-hour float this stretch has many islands and back channels to probe with a fly.

2. Policeman's Flats - McKinnon Flats (24km/15miles). This float is the Bows' most popular. You will encounter many different water types. Deep pools, choppy runs, riffles, and gentle glides are a predominant features of this section. Sun baked cliffs are numerous and come alive with the sound of grasshoppers come August.

3. McKinnon Flats - Carseland Weir. The closer you travel to the weir the more the river backs up and braids into endless backwater channels. This water can be very challenging for the beginner or expert, but if you like to stalk individual fish with dry flies, this is the place for you. Try not to jump out of your waders as one of our unseen, resident, beavers slaps his tail right beside you in the fading light.

Vehicle shuttle service is available, and recommended, due to the long distances between boat launches. Barb McDonald, at South Bow Shuttle (403) 271-7756) provides reliable service and up to date fishing information.

If you are planning a trip to the Bow (whether you plan to be guided or not) it is best to contact a reliable outfitter or fly shop. The newly founded Fly Fishing Outfitters Association of Alberta has links to shops and outfitters. They can be reached at (403) 271-7756 or view the web site at http://www.cadvision.com/foaa.

Kendra Konkin

Fishing a log jam on a southern Alberta stream

Don Reilly, founder and primary guide of Alpine Anglers, based in Banff, and offering trips, specializing on the upper Bow River, and the Upper Oldman and Livingstone Rivers of the Eastern Slopes. Walk-and-wade and float trips from 1/2 day to multiple day excursions. Casting and fishing instructions are available as well. Don has authored articles for the Banff weekly newspaper, the Crag and Canyon, and provided editorial advice for other tourism publications.

Don has been an avid fly fisherman on the Bow River below Calgary since 1978, and in the Banff-Canmore area since 1987. He has also fished the Crowsnest and Oldman system for over 10 years. Don was the founding member of the Upper Bow Valley chapter of Trout Unlimited Canada. He was past president of the chapter, and member of the Board of Directors of the Alberta Council of Trout Unlimited Chapters.

Smaller Trophy Streams of Alberta
Don Reilly

"The great spine of the mountains pushing its way boldly through the thin skin of the western prairie, that range we call the Rockies, harbors the greatest trout fishery in the world ..... There are sweeping rivers, tiny brooks, inviting streams, not to mention a host of lakes and ponds, each with its own character ..." (Gary Borger).

The region of Alberta known as the southern east slopes contains some of the most beautiful, and unspoiled streams in the province. Fishing them is a joy, and should be considered a treat.

The upper reaches of the Oldman River, Livingstone River, and their tributaries all originate high in the Rocky Mountains, near the Continental Divide along the eastern edges of these magnificent mountains. These are predominantly cutthroat, bull trout, and rocky mountain whitefish streams.

Access to these streams is by way of Highway 940, "the forestry trunk road", which extends from highway 3, in the south to Grand Prairie in the north. There is no accommodation available between the southern end and the northern section for this article (Highwood Junction). There are, however, a few official campgrounds, and many "wilderness", user-maintained camping areas. Some of these are truly spectacular, even without toilets, picnic tables, or fire rings. Keep an eye open for any two track path departing the road and follow at your wim. Remember that these are 'user maintained' areas, so pack out everything (human waste included). Please use these areas with respect of the environment and others. The attraction of these areas is their wildness. Use and enjoy and leave it for the next guy!

The forestry trunk road is a well maintained gravel road, which is graded fairly regularly, but may be a bit on the rough side. For most of its length it parallels either the Oldman or Livingstone River, sharing a narrow north-south valley.

Both the Livingstone and upper Oldman are classic alpine freestone streams. They vary from fast, tumbling, turbulent rapids 6 to 20 feet wide, and 1 to 6 feet deep, to slow deep pools ranging to 30-60 feet long, up to 30 feet wide, and 15 or more feet deep. Lots of good fish holding water. Some great fishing.

All of these streams have decent populations of Golden stone flies, green drakes, both of which hatch in mid summer, and lesser

139

hatches of pale morning duns, Adam's, caddis, and a few other mayflies. These are a dry fly fishers paradise, with the cutts rising greedily during time of the hatches. The perfect presentation of the perfect fly is not a prerequisite. Typical fly fishing equipment consists of 4, 5, or 6 weight rods in 7 1/2 to 9 feet in length. Most of this water is quite small, and casts of more than 40 to 60 feet are seldom required. A floating line will suffice for almost all of the fishing circumstances encountered.

For dry flies, leaders of 7 to 9 feet tapering to 6X will suffice. When using streamers, shorter and heavier 5 to 6 feet and 4X are more appropriate due to the heavier hits you'll encounter. Leaders 9 to 15 feet long, tapering to 3X or 4X, work well for nymphing. My personal rig is a 12 foot leader set up with two nymphs tied in series. The first is tied normally to the leader. A piece of tippet 2 to 3 feet long is then tied in at the bend and the second, heavier, fly tied to this. Split shot, if necessary, is added about 12" above the second fly. A decent sized strike indicator is needed to stay afloat with all of this weight, and the rig can be hard to cast. False casting is not recommended. A lobbing cast works really well, for the relatively short casts of these smaller rivers. Vary the position of the indicator to keep the flies near the bottom.

Just as the annual floods recede, which typically last from late May to mid June, the season opens, and the stone flies are hatching. Large nymphs fished deep can be particularly effective. So, too, can large dry flies like Improved Sofa Pillows and Stimulators. Fishing these huge dries is really easy, even for those with less than perfect eye sight. What a treat to watch a trout slide out from its holding spot and smack your fly. Fish on!

Early July, and the green drakes are hatching. This is the second great hatch of the season for these waters, and happens at a time of year when days are long, skies are blue, evenings are warm, and the flows are decreasing. Fish are now accustomed to looking up, and voraciously rise to a well presented green drake imitation. There are actually two green drake hatches. The earlier Western Green Drake is the larger 8's and 10's being adequate. The latter Small Western Green Drake 12's hatch from mid July to mid August.

Hoppertunity time. Oh, what a time!! Much of the upper Oldman and Livingstone River Valley is leased to ranchers for grazing, that means grass, and that folks, means hoppers, and that means fun.

Late summer and early fall can be beautiful in the foothill country. Nights are cool, with frost not uncommon, and days can be out and out hot. Temperatures can reach 25 degrees Celsius. It is my favorite time of year in the valley. Elk can be heard beguiling as you fish.

The year 1998 sees some significant changes to the regulations pertaining to the East Slope fisheries.

1. Open seasons have been standardized for each east slopes fisheries units, which correspond to the watershed. All of the waters discussed here are within ES1 which is the Bow River drainage. All flowing water is open from June 16 to October 31, unless otherwise noted in the regulations.

2. Limits have been reduced to 2 trout and or grayling and 5 whitefish.

3. More streams or sections of streams have been designated as no kill, or catch and release. All of the Livingstone is no kill for all species. Check the regs for the Oldman and tributaries.

4. Size limits have been changed (increased). Again, check the regs.

5. Bait restrictions have been imposed for all trout and grayling. Limited use of maggots is allowed in specified water only.

6. Barbless is dead. Alberta Fish and Wildlife states that because there is a lack of conclusive evidence that barbless reduces mortality the requirement for barbless hooks has been removed from the regulations. I personally disagree with this decision, although I do not argue with the mortality issue. I firmly believe that barbless hooks make removal much easier, thereby reducing handling time and stress levels. Barbless hooks do much less physical damage to the fish by leaving a smaller wound. In my humble opinion, either of these arguments alone is sufficient to keep barbless as a policy, combining both makes it ridiculous to remove the barbless clause. Needless to say I strongly encourage everyone to go barbless. Fishing is a sport, and being sporting means doing the least possible harm.

Rainbow Trout and The Crowsnest River
Jeff Mironuck

Coming from my home in Cranbrook B.C., the Crowsnest is only a couple hours away. The thought of fly fishing for those chunky rainbows is enough to make almost anyone want to get away from the steady hard pulling of cutthroat trout that are so common to the Kootenays. I don't want anyone to get the wrong impression of cutthroat. They are great to angle for and their beauty is almost unsurpassable. The strong fight and their willingness to take a fly, make the cutthroat a fly fisher's trout. However, the fight of a cutthroat simply cannot be compared to the wild, energetic and sometimes aerobic actions of a fighting rainbow. The Crowsnest river is full of these trout.

One of my first trips to the Crowsnest River started off as a beautiful spring day filled with mayflies in the air and a strong sense of promise. I was with Pete Morrison, a good fishermen and friend. We tossed around the idea of angling under Lundbreck Falls but with the traffic there we drove farther down the river. The cool air made walking easy and with our waders on and all our gear we half slid, half walked down the steep bank to the river bottom. Since the trout did not seem to be taking mayflies on the surface we opted for nymphs. The Crowsnest is a scenic wadeable river that seems almost as if God designed it for fly fishing. The morning flew by quickly as we carried on down stream searching for rising trout. After a couple early hours, I only brought a brookie to the bank with a weighted Pheasant Tail. Pete and I were both changing flies and the selection in all of our boxes was slowly dwindling. Then "magic hour" hit for us. A small caddis scraped along a back eddy just long enough for me to judge its size and color before being engulfed by a large rainbow. Pete reached into his box of dries and surfaced with a small sedge. Instantly upon hitting the water he was into a feisty 18 incher. What followed that day was a great learning experience. It was a little more complicated than "caddis fishing". We had to copy the fly exactly. Color was just as important as size, not just any pattern would do. As the sun began to lower the fishing heated up. At one time I had the same trout rise to my fly over 12 times before being hooked. (not a real bright fish) We lost count after a dozen or so each. Many fish were large and brilliantly colored. It was one of my most memorable experiences river fishing and I'm sure Pete feels the same way. The ride home was a good one that day.

Renowned as one of the finest fly fishing rivers in Alberta, the Crowsnest River flows east and is easily accessible from highway 3. Rainbow trout are predominate in the river and some browns can be found below the falls. Dainty Tricos and huge hoppers all have their place at one time or another on the Crowsnest. Blessed with much fishable water, anglers can be spread throughout its length. Most of the angling pressure is felt below Lundbreck and crowds can form during the peak times.

Located in south western Alberta this medium sized water provides quality year-round angling. Wading is a must to fish the Crowsnest properly. The river flows out of Crowsnest Lake near the Alberta-British Columbia border and continues its journey as a free stone stream until reaching the Old Man Dam Reservoir. Hatches of mayflies, stone flies and caddis flies give the fly fisher some ideas of what to use when nymphing or fishing the dry fly. The upper section of the river generally has smaller fish in the 10-14 inch range. Here you will find rainbows, cutthroat and brookies. Below the falls in the lower section the fish get much larger. 16-18 inch fish are average with many caught over 18 inches regularly.

The angling season usually begins mid-June after runoff. Good searching patterns down deep such as a Pheasant Tail can be a excellent early season fly. When the fish are active on the surface, an array of midges or even some mayflies can be effective. I like to try mayflies as often as possible when fishing the early season stream. Even though a hatch may not be occurring at that time, some fish are always scanning the water for that odd lone dun. Anglers flock to the Crowsnest each June in hopes of experiencing the amazing salmon fly hatch. Large dark stone fly nymphs represent a very good sized meal for trout and the fly fisher can imitate these easily. Although the major emergence occurs early in the year these nymphs are active in the stream all year. In the right conditions the nymphs will crawl out from the water and emerge into the large salmon fly adult. Like the name indicates, the color of these adults is primarily a pink-salmon combination. Large Stimulators can imitate the stone flies in this stage. At this time of they year trout can be very selective. Often strong hatches of mayflies can go unnoticed by the trout when they are keyed in on the stone flies. It's important to be very aware of everything available to the trout when fishing the Crowsnest.

As summer begins the water level begins to drop and most anglers turn to dry fly fishing. Caddis, mayflies and stone flies all have their moments on the water. Terrestrial fishing can be excellent with hoppers leading the way. The summer clarity of the Crowsnest can cause the trout to be wary and at the same time some fish will travel great distances to feed. Wading becomes even easier and the fish are still very active. Streamer patterns can draw out the larger fish at times and when the fishing does slow down they may be interested in a small nymph fished deep. Nymph fishing is very important as the fish get much attention and the deeper pools are more attractive to them.

September is one of the best months. Everyone's back to work and school while the trout are busy bulking up for the upcoming winter. Although the trout have seen many flies over the year, the right one can still bring plenty of fish to the net. Blue-winged olive mayflies and some terrestrials can still do the trick although I prefer nymphing most of the time.

Both Coleman and Blairmore host a variety of motels and campgrounds. A nice campground can be found at Lundbreck falls although it can be busy. Whenever you are able to get to the Crowsnest, the fish will most likely be there waiting for you. From early spring to late fall the Crowsnest fish are a joy to catch. Remember to check up on the current regs and always practice catch and release.

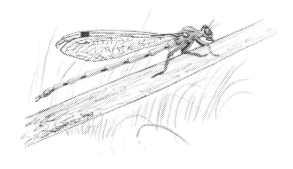

Frank Wood

Photo courtesy of the Edmonton Sun

Frank Wood developed an early addiction to fly fishing at age 13, fishing for brook trout in Prince Edward Island. Originally born in Belleville, Ontario his malady intensified upon moving to Edmonton, Alberta in 1979, and discovering the Blue-ribbon trout waters there. He currently is employed as an Aircraft Planner with SPAR Aerospace Limited and as the fly fishing instructor with Edmonton Public Schools.

Frank owns Streamside Adventures, a guided fly fishing business based out of Edmonton taking clients into the best trout streams throughout Alberta. He has a particular love for the cutthroat trout of the North Ram River and Arctic grayling of the Little Smoky River. In January 1998, Frank became the first and only person in Alberta to be Nationally Certified as a Freshwater Fishing Guide.

He is a past member of Trout Unlimited, The Edmonton Trout Fishing Club, and The Federation of Fly Fishers. He currently is an active member of the executive with the Alberta Sport Fishing Industry Association. Aside from guiding and fishing, he spends his "spare time" with his wife Jodi and future fly fishers Brynne and Jenna in Edmonton, or at the family ranch in Ponoka. For a guided trip Frank can be reached at 403-475-9297 or email him at woodf@oanet.com.

North Ram River
Frank Wood

This river means one thing to me, I can breathe again. Perhaps it's because of the physical distance separating me from my home water. The river is 367 km SW of Edmonton, making it too far for a day trip. Perhaps it is the whole North Ram River experience itself that will cause me to rush madly about; sacrificing regular jobs and marital relations for the chance to head back down and fish it again. All I know is that once I have turned the ignition off on the truck; and am staring at the river through the windshield, I let out a deep breath and say to myself "I made it home".

I first fished the North Ram River on the 2nd of July 1988. Up to this point in my fly fishing career I fished mostly lakes, and some foothill trout streams such as Prairie and Shunda Creeks. The limit of my big water experiences was drifting the Lower Bow River. Although I like the Lower Bow; I am a walk and wade kind of guy, and I yearned for a freestone river in the mountains that was free of drift boats.

I had heard rumors about the quality of the river's cutthroat trout fishery during meetings of the Edmonton Trout Fishing Club, where small groups would huddle together in the back shadows of the classroom and talk in quick hushed whispers. As the stories continued, the participants would get a glazed look in their eyes, indicating that the current "hot spot" had been discovered.

I happened upon one of these conversations while sitting with a group of my friends; collectively known as "the predators" due to their fly fishing prowess. They told me that they were going to the North Ram River to fish on the July long weekend, and asked if I wanted to come along. I wasn't able to join them for the whole weekend; but agreed to meet them in Nordegg on Saturday morning for a day of fishing.

I departed from Rimbey on the morning of the second of July, and drove to Nordegg to meet the predators. After exchanging pleasantries, and pausing for a stretch; we drove south on the Forestry Trunk Road to the river. The drive down was exciting enough, as I got to play chase car to the lead predator driving his Landcruiser at top speed. In spite of the blur of the passing landscape, I was quite taken by the combination of a high grade gravel road winding through the forested front ranges.

We arrived at our access spot, geared up and then proceeded to hike one and one-half hours downstream and fished our way back to where we started. Looking back on that first trip, I could have avoided the grueling pace that the lead predator kept up on the hike if I'd known that some of the best fishing spots are accessible right from the side of the road.

When I started fishing the river after resting up from the hike, I was a little intimidated by the speed of the current. It appeared that no sooner had I cast my fly, it was dragging in the current directly downstream of me. It took a while for me to get used to the drifts and the wading, but by the end of the day, I didn't even notice it anymore.

One word described the water as I fished the river, textbook. It was as if someone had taken the pages out of a book on reading the water, and laid them out in front of me. There were many combinations of pools, riffles, and runs. In fact there was too much good water for the neophyte fly fisher, and I know that my sloppy approach and presentation put down plenty of fish.

After all was said and done, I only caught two cutthroat trout. The first one was a fourteen incher that was coming out from underneath the branch of a submerged tree periodically to sip in a mayfly. How I cast my yellow Humpy up tight enough to the branch without snagging the fly; I don't know, but it worked and I hooked him. It appeared to me that the rise was in slow motion and the fish had a golden sheen to it. In fact this wasn't just the view of a incurable romanticist, but a phenomena that occurs when the fish rises from the depths and the water is clear.

Number two was taken when I was nymphing a beautiful pool. I bounced a Bitch Creek nymph down the steps that formed the head of the pool, and felt my arm jar as a sixteen inch "Cut" soundly took my imitation, and made off for the tail end. After a good fight I admired him briefly before releasing him. I was quite taken by the beauty of these Westslope cutthroat; and have never been able to take a picture that adequately depicts their wonderful colors as displayed in the water. Up to this point, my favorite trout was the brookie, but in one day's fishing it had been displaced to number two.

One thing you notice about the North Ram, is how out in the open you are. We were about three-quarters of the way back to the vehicles, when I saw thunderheads off in the distance to the west. I said my good-byes to the predators, and gumbooted it back to the car. The thunderstorms hit half way back to Nordegg, and I was quite fortunate in my timing as the driving rain was starting to wash out the sides of the road on the north side of the North Saskatchewan valley.

I relaxed a bit once I reached Nordegg, and stopped for some gas and a quick phone call to my wife. I grossly underestimated my arrival time back in Rimbey, but the trip passed quickly for me as I replayed the events of the first day on my newly discovered North Ram River and planned for my return visit home.

The North Ram River is the story of a fishery that never was. A preliminary Biological Survey of the river in 1952 turned up only Longnose Dace (Miller/Paetz). The survey recommended the introduction of cutthroat trout and Rocky Mountain whitefish. Westslope cutthroat trout from south eastern B.C. were first stocked in the river in 1955. This was followed up by repeat stockings in 1961 and 1970.

After the river was first stocked, fishing was allowed on odd numbered years. However, angling pressure was intensive during open years, contributing to stock depletion. As a result, catch and release regulations were placed on the river and its tributaries in 1982. The cutthroat trout have been thriving under these regulations, with catch rates as high as 4 to 6 fish per hour. The opportunity to catch a 50 cm cutthroat trout is very real on this river.

The North Ram River originates in the Ram Mountains of western Alberta. It flows east for 50 km where it joins the Ram River. It is a freestone river with many pools spaced far enough apart that one has time to enjoy a few wild strawberries while walking between them. The river opens to angling in the middle of June, and the best fishing is from the July to the September long weekends. There is a runoff from the snowpack in the spring, but it is usually finished by open season. The river is susceptible to heavy rains in the last two weeks in June, but generally it takes a day for the water to clear up after the rain has ceased.

The main tributaries are Joyce and Cripple Creeks. On average, the cutthroats in the tributaries are smaller but more forgiving than the main river. Joyce Creek in particular is extremely accessible, offering some wonderful angling for the young or inexperienced due to its smaller size.

There are many well worn trails winding through the Spruce and Lodgepole Pine that dominate the area, making for a easy walk and a break from the heat of the sun in summer. Part of the reason for the trails, are the ever present cattle that meander through the bush, the area downstream of the trunk road is a grazing lease.

The whole corridor is rich in other wildlife, as one has the opportunity to see moose, wolf, elk, Mule deer, Ruffed and Spruce grouse. Of course one can expect to see squirrels, chipmunks and Gray jays around the campsite.

The North Ram river can be accessed from the west by taking Highway 93 (Icefields Parkway) until it intersects Highway 11 (David Thompson). Drive east on hwy 11 until you reach Secondary Road 940 (Forestry Trunk Road). Head south for 32 km and you will come to the forestry campsite on the banks of the North Ram River. To access the river form the east, take highway 2 until it intersects highway 11. Drive west on hwy 11 until you reach Secondary Road 940. Head south for 32 km. Be prepared to make it a weekend trip when fishing this river, as the distance from Edmonton is 367 km, making it too far for a day trip.

Motel accommodation is available in Nordegg, Rocky Mountain House and near the Saskatchewan Crossing in the Icefields Parkway. Several good forestry campgrounds are scattered through the Nordegg area on highway 11, as well as on the Forestry Trunk Road. There also is a gas station and general store located in Nordegg.

Derek Bird with a Kootenay River cutthroat

Friends, and the Little Smoky River
Frank Wood

I used to hunt birds during the months of September and October in Alberta's Parkland areas. I started this habit after I moved to Alberta in 1979, with my good friend Ron Anderson. How we survived these trips is the subject matter of other stories, but Ron was transferred to Ontario and I started hunting with my negotiating adversary from work, Gary Wolfe. He too was transferred. I had one more hunting partner left. My fly fishing mentor Bob Cormier. This also ended as he took on a project to illustrate a book on mayflies. He would collect his specimens during our summer fishing trips, and start his preliminary sketches in September. I was either going to have to find new friends to hunt with, or go it alone. There were other factors that came into play when I decided to quit. The amount of time I spent fly fishing started to skyrocket, while the amount of time I spent at home developing lasting marital memories started to decline. It was also around this time that we were expecting our first child, so I knew that something had to give, and it wasn't going to be the fishing.

Up to this point, my fishing season naturally ended when my hunting season started. This wasn't the case anymore. The river fly fishing opportunities around Edmonton in the fall were mostly limited to chucking streamers for browns. This is not my style, and I found myself feeling pangs of regret when it came time to pack away the rod and gear for the season. I thought that if I could have one more really good day, the memories themselves would carry me through the long winter months.

I found an opportunity to have regretless closure of my fly fishing season in the form of the Little Smoky River. Carl Hunt, Regional Fisheries Biologist from Edson gave a presentation to the Edmonton Trout Fishing Club one winter night about Arctic grayling fishing in Alberta. I had already been exposed to them in the Wildhay River, but this experience had only left me wondering if there was anywhere in Alberta where a stable population of decent size (36 cm +) grayling still existed. Then Carl talked about the Little Smoky's unique fishery. Well now, that got my attention. I even moved closer to the front of the classroom, so I could hear and retain every word that Carl spoke. I assaulted Carl with several questions after the presentation, and left that meeting determined to fish the river as soon as possible.

At this time I started to make a new friend. His name was Gary Schaupmeyer. I had known him as a fellow Trout Club member for some time, but until that winter when our paths crossed at an ice-fishing course, we hadn't really fished together. Gary taught me that I didn't need to treat each fly fishing outing as a personal race against the clock. He taught me how to be comfortable with the whole experience and relax and enjoy it. I also learned that Gary had fished the Little Smoky previously, more importantly he knew where to go. The only thing left to do was coordinate our social schedules.

On the morning of October 7th 1994, we piled our gear into Gary's van (a little later than anticipated), and headed Northwest to fish the river for the weekend. The drive to Fox Creek was a long one, but we were rested up and our eagerness to fish the river prompted plenty of conversation along the way. After a leisurely stop for breakfast, we made the last leg of our journey down to Grizzly Junction.

When we arrived, I thought I recognized a certain Landcruiser parked there. I then saw the predators gearing up for a days fishing, and after exchanging pleasantries; we decided to all fish together. After a brief hike we arrived at our fishing spot for the day. It was a deep run about 45 metres long. I couldn't believe it. How could this stretch of water provide enough fishing for a group of 5 serious fly fisherman. Well it did. We fished the run all day within metres of each other, only leaving the water when the cold started to make our toes hurt, or in Gary's case when he felt a nap coming on.

The fishing in a word, was fantastic. It did, however, start out a little slow. We couldn't get the grayling to rise to a dry fly (small wonder due to the cold water temperature), but Gary was using a Bead Head Hare's Ear nymph and doing quite well. Not to long after that, the grayling started to rise to our Adam's Irresistible's and we caught one after another. The only pause in the action was when we took the time to tie on a fresh fly, although we caught quite a few grayling on "drowned" imitations.

From start to finish I caught and released 72 grayling ranging in size from 33 to 48 cm long. Many of the fish would come clear out of the water to take the fly, as well jump several times after being hooked. All in all it was a magical day, and one that I will never forget. Gary and I fished the same stretch of the river the next day, and only caught a little over 20 grayling apiece. Little wonder since some of the fish were no doubt suffering from a sore mouth since the day before.

To prove that my first day on the river wasn't a fluke, I have fished it many times since and had the same results in many different sections. After having a day or two like this on the Little Smoky River in the second week in October, I don't have a problem hanging up my rod for the season - regret free.

The story of the Little Smoky Fishery is one of success. The river has produced incredible fishing for grayling and bull trout for many years, but unlike the rivers of the Athabasca system to the south, the fishery is still intact. One of the reasons is accessibility. Only recently has the oil and timber industries opened up the area through development, allowing the average person to access the river with a regular passenger vehicle. I also believe that the traveling required to get there (330 km from Edmonton), has been enough to discourage a casual trip to the river.

The other main reason is that the river has had many friends and guardians who have recognized its unique fishery and the potential for over-exploitation. Darryl Smith and members of the Valleyview Fish and Game Association, as well as many other organizations successfully lobbied the provincial government for special regulations to protect the fishery. In 1989 the government responded by designating the upper 96 km of the river as catch and release. 1996 saw the catch and release area extended another 20 km downstream.

The grayling are thriving under these regulations with catch rates as high as 7 to 11 fish per hour. The opportunity to catch 10 to 15 fish per day that exceed 30 cm in length is very real on this river. As an added bonus, there are some truly huge bull trout lurking in the shadows ready to make a run at a well placed streamer, or the occasional hooked grayling.

The Little Smoky River originates in the Boreal foothills east of Grande Cache. There are extensive muskeg areas with springs in the upper stretches of the river; feeding into it and giving the water a tint similar to the color of weak tea. The river flows for 155 km before it enters the Smoky River, a tributary to the Peace River. The river opens to angling in the middle of June, and the best fishing, at least for big grayling is from the end of August until the second or third week in October.

There are many trails winding through the Lodgepole Pine and White Aspen that dominate the area, paralleling the river and provide innumerable fishing opportunities. The whole area is rich in wildlife other than fish, with the opportunity to view Moose, Wolf, Elk, Black and Grizzly Bears, White-tailed and Mule Deer, and Ruffed Grouse. Of course, expect to see Gray Jays and Squirrels around the campsites.

The Little Smoky River can be accessed by taking the Amoco-Bigstone Road 30 km SW of Fox Creek. There is a forestry camp-ground at Smoke Lake, and primitive campsites at Grizzly Junction and Tony Creek. Motel accommodation is available in Fox Creek, Whitecourt and Valleyview. There are also many gas stations and food stores located in these towns.

Bob Cormier fighting a cutthroat on the North Ram River

Top Lakes in South Western Alberta
Stew Slymon

Chester Lake

From the summit of Mt. Chester I peered through the mist down the impressive east wall into the deep inkwell of Chester Lake and thought back to the first time I had fished its shores. For some time I had heard the rumors. Rumors of Arctic Char being planted and reaching a good size. Arctic Char I thought, "well you haven't caught an Arctic Char before." The trail from the road-head to the lake is a good workout. Almost 5 kilometers long and an elevation gain of 300 meters. After many switch-backs and several blasts screeching from my bear whistle, I approached the open glade that led down to the lake. I stopped to scout things out, there was a slight breeze and a resultant ripple on the water made the approach less of a concern. Calm conditions would have required a more stealth-like approach as most mountain lakes are gun clear. Fish can be quite spooky as they cruise the shallow perimeters looking for food. As I approached the water I immediately spotted small clusters of may-fly duns wind-surfing on the surface. An occasional splash of a small fish also suggested that the bugs were being intercepted before they were able to take off on their short trip with destiny. Bad for the bugs but good for me. I stepped back from the shore and anxiously strung my rod. I tied on one of my favorite dry fly patterns for the Callibaetis adults. The Adam's hit the water and was immediately engulfed. The small fish put up a good scrap and as I netted it I noticed the bright red slash on the fill cover. A nice little alpine cutthroat, but not an Arctic Char. Several cuts later I thought "well, maybe the char are hanging out in the deeper water." The hatch stopped and forced me to change flies. I don't like to mess with success so I stayed with the Callibaetis but switched to a nymph and an intermediate line. With this combination I was able to explore the deeper water. Within an hour I had netted 4 or 5 larger cuts but I was beginning to think that the rumor of Arctic Char was strictly that, rumor. A change in the wind and I had to hike over to the east shore. The steep slope plummeted straight into the water with virtually no shallow transition zone. I fired a cast parallel to the shore about six feet out. I counted to five before starting my retrieve. Nothing. The next cast I let sink for a count of fifteen. On about my third pull I was surprised by a good hard hit. As the struggle wore on I noticed two things. The fish was bigger than the others and it seemed to fight differently. Was this the infamous Arctic Char I had been hoping for? Well, it certainly wasn't a cutthroat but I wasn't sure it was an Arctic Char either. It looked more like a lake trout to me (also a char by the way) but supposedly there were no lakers in Chester Lake. I only caught the one Arctic Char that day but was satisfied that I could add another species to my fly caught list. A couple of years later the Arctic Char came off my list as I found out that a study of the lake suggested that these fish were in fact Northern Dolly Varden (also a Char! Confused yet?) and not after all the mythical Arctics. But hey, the Dollies are in fact rare individuals themselves and certainly gives the angler more than a good reason to visit Chester Lake.

Picklejar Lakes

With a name like Picklejar Lakes who wouldn't want to fish there? I had driven by the sign on Highway 40 many times. The lakes had been closed to fishing for many years. Some said it was because of the pure strain of East Slope cutthroat trout that lived in these lakes and the Government was using them as a hatchery. Whatever the reason, I was curious and decided to visit these lakes without a fly rod. On my first visit I made the mistake of thrashing up Picklejar Creek. It turned out to be a bushwhacking nightmare but the payoff was four of the most jewel like lakes I had ever encountered. Situated at the entrance of a large mountain cirque, it is a magical place. The fish were there too, cruising the shallows in pairs and threes, I knew I would return. On my next visit I found an easier way into the lakes. By hiking up Lantern Creek just to the south the walk in time was reduced to about 2 to 2.5 hours on good game trails. It was at least 3 of 4 visits to the lakes before the ban on fishing was lifted. I almost felt guilty when I hooked the fish and watched it swim away I decided my fishing day was over, I had accomplished what I had set out to do and I didn't need to catch anymore.

Gap Lake

My daydream was rudely interrupted when the fish smacked the fly hard. The run began slowly but as soon as I started to apply line pressure he took off like a rocket. Fifty meters into my backing I though " big fish ". I had moved over to the west shore of the lake to take advantage of the steep scree slope and use it as a windbreak. I had been casting blind for some time and had let my mind wander to the buttress of rock towering over me on Grotto Mountain dominating the view on this side of the lake. Three more long runs and the big fish began to tire. As I slowly brought the fish closer to the tube I finally started to realize how big he was. It was indeed a Gap Lake brown and a large one at that! The huge male had as big a kiped jaw as I had seen on any fresh water fish. I slid him up on the apron of my tube by his huge tail to get an accurate measurement. At just under 28 inches it was truly a trophy brown. Its almost golden color was highlighted by red ringed spots on his huge flank. I slowly slipped him back into the water and a couple of minutes later he was ready to be released. Gap Lake is one of those alpine lakes that can be accessed by car. In fact the 1A highway almost forms its northern shore. Gap Lake is an odd place, basically it is a low spot between the Base of Grotto Mountain and the Bow River which flows less than a kilometer from where you park the car. You can't see the river but its there across the lake on the other side of the railway tracks that run along the south shore of the lake. The Bow is so close to this shore that a culvert was built under the railway tracks allowing the lake to drain into the river. This access to the river explains the brown trout that have used the lake's outlet as a back-door entrance to the lake. There are not a lot of brown's here, a two fish day would be considered a good day. If the browns are not cooperating then maybe the large Rocky Mountain whitefish that also inhabit the lake should be considered as they are sporting fish and the Alberta record for this species of 5lbs. 10.5 oz. came out of Gap Lake in 1991. The Lake overall is quite shallow and when the wind comes up, which it can do quickly, the chop can be quite rough.

Barnaby Ridge Lakes/Southfork Lakes

A hike-in group of lakes via a steep 5 km trail. Well worth the effort as the lakes are laden with gold! Gold that is in the form of the rare and beautiful Golden trout. I have only visited these lakes once and did not have an opportunity to fish as we were hit with a nasty snow, hail and electric storm. But as McCarthy said, " I shall return". Check with local Fish and Wildlife office before setting off as this is prime Grizzly bear habitat and they will have the latest and greatest on bear activity. A good side trip if you are fishing the Crowsnest River.

Lower Kananaskis Lake

This is a large alpine lake that is car accessible. It takes time to explore this lake but is worth the effort. It holds a variety of fish from rainbows, cutts and brook trout, to the rare bull trout. The bull trout (again a char) record for Alberta came from this lake and these fish can be taken with the right fly and the right selection of fly lines. I prefer the Lower Kananaskis Lake to the Upper Lake, mainly due to the chance of catching larger fish. Both lakes have good boat access and both have speed limitations. Excellent camping facilities are nearby.

Hector Lake

The fish hit the small leech violently, but then as quickly as the fish started to gain momentum, the line stopped dead. " Damn", I thought, "broke me off". As I started to retrieve the line back to replace the fly I was startled when the line suddenly ripped out of my hand and started to head west with little regard to the 3X tippet that separated us. I knew I was in for a long struggle. My antics with the big fish soon drew some attention, and close to twenty-five minutes later, as I finally tailed the chiseled beauty and pulled her up on the apron, I heard the "oohs" and "ahhs" of the half dozen or so anglers and canoeists that had congregated around me. "I've caught a lot of salmon smaller than that", some yelled, and after confirming the length at 29.5 inches, I thought "Yes, and so have I". At well over 12 pounds it was my largest fly-caught rainbow and a fitting example of the trophy fish found at Hector Lake.

Hector Lake is a private fishery. Similar to other pay as you go fisheries, like the Douglas Lake Ranch in south central British Columbia, and a growing number in the U.S. Located on the Morley Indian Reserve a short distance west of Calgary, the lake is maintained as a trophy fishery. Strict catch and release rules are in effect, as well a bait ban. Both gas and electric motors and prohibited. As of this writing, there was a severe winterkill on this lake (the result of malfunctioning aeration equipment during the winter of 1996/97). Fish were reintroduced very early in the spring of 1997 and by the fall they were coming along nicely and had reached lengths of 17-18 inches. A number of brood stock were also thrown in so there are some nice surprises as well! It will be a couple of years before this lake can be reclassified as a trophy fishery but it is still worth a visit as the location itself is worth the cost, which by the way is currently $20.00 per day. For those willing to pay the $20.00, don't expect the fish to be easy, they are not. The fish here are as challenging as any trophy lake I have fished and the well-equipped lake angler would be wise to carry a full selection of lake patterns. Hector Lake is very nutrient-rich and has good healthy populations of chironomids, damsels, dragons, caddis and mayflies, as well as scuds, backswimmers, leeches and terrestrials. The lake is shallow with a maximum depth of maybe 20 feet, but on average you won't be fishing in much more than 10 feet of water. The lake is not big and can be fished from a tube quite easily. Before setting out for the lake, phone the Nakoda Lodge at 1-403-881-3949 for the latest information.

Dipping Vat Lake

I had to go there. Again it was the name of this lake that initially attracted me. It also had the reputation of being one of Alberta's most nutrient-rich lakes and held some very large fish. Well, I certainly confirmed the nutrient richness of the lake on my first visit when I backed out of the water, climbed out of my tube and discovered my waders had been replaced by a writhing swarm of biomass. Every square inch of my neoprenes was inhabited by scuds, most of them, were the larger gammarus variety, hundreds, if not thousands, well over an inch long. As it turned out (not surprisingly) I didn't even touch a fish that day and have similar results on return visits. What brings me back from time to time are two things. The fact that the lake is so biodiverse makes it an amazing place to observe and learn about the entomology of lakes in general. The hatches I have witnessed on this lake are the most prolific I have ever seen. I have taken these observations back to the tying bench and it has helped me to become a better angler. It is truly a great outdoor classroom. Reason #2? I've finally managed to catch some of those large Dipping Vat rainbows.

Police Outpost Lake

The ice had only been off for a week and the wind had picked up substantially since leaving home. I knew my best bet would be to find a place out of the direct wind and shallow enough to have the temperature needed to activate some fish into feeding. The final entrance to the lake sits high above it and allows a perfect spot to scope out the lake and determine the best possibilities. As it turned out, the most protected spot was a small bay right in front of the boat launch. A good chironomid hatch was under way as I slipped my tube into the water and it was not long before my little 4 wt. was being tested by some of the lake's chunky rainbows and brookies. These were not large fish but it was almost a fish-a-cast and it had been a long winter so I was grateful for the day. Not only that, but Police Outpost is an aesthetically pleasing body of water and offers the fly fisher plenty of opportunities. The view of Chief Mountain just over the international border in the state of Montana is worth the price of admission. The lake is also the centerpiece for a provincial park and has a large, well-maintained campground. Best fished during the week as it does get crowded on weekends during the season.

Lees Lake

A fun place to fish and a great place to learn the art of fishing from a float tube, and a great place to take kids. Generally speaking, expect smaller fish but lots of them. There are also a few surprises for the more advanced angler.

Mami/Paine Lake

Fairly large body of water directly east of the gates to Waterton National Park. If the lake has not had a large winterkill, some nice fish can be had. Nice campground and boat launch facilities.

Badger Lake

I had paddled my tube for a kilometer to the edge of the weed bed I wanted to fish. I had some success catching and releasing two fish in the 10-15 lb. Range on the outer edges of the weed bed. I slowly worked myself into the heart of the weed mass and found a perfect channel. I anchored at the far e end of this six-foot wide trough and fired a cast about 50 feet along its length. I was only in five feet of water so I did not let the fly sink very long before starting my retrieve. After my third or fourth pull I saw the golden/white flash of an under belly followed immediately by a very large boil that resembled a small tidal wave. The fish inhaled the fly and instantly took off at right angle to my rod. I lifted the tip hard, set the hook and immediately applied pressure to try and keep the giant head out of the weeds as it slashed along the surface. Luck was on my side as the fish chose his line of flight poorly and headed towards more open water where I was able to control him far easier than if he had headed into the heavy cabbage. After twenty minutes of slogging it out with the monster pike, I slipped a coil of nylon rope around its broad tail, tightened up and then proceeded to extract the fly and measure its length. At 46 and a half inches I indeed had a Badger Lake monster, one of three I was to catch this day. Badger Lake is an amazing pike fishery. If it were located in the Northwest Territories, Babe Winkleman would have made it a household name by now. Badger Lake is actually a reservoir, one of which promotes the fast growth of the bait fish that the pike feed upon. The lake has a large shoreline and although there are a fair number of hardware fishermen that frequent the lake, you can easily find a spot to call your own. Badger is a fairly big lake and is best fished with a small boat and motor.

Travers Reservoir

I watched as the pelican swallowed the large dead fish whole. The bloated carcass was being washed out into the middle of the bay by the current formed as the thunderous volume of water raced down the spillway. The birds would swoop down, land at the bottom of the spillway and proceed to ride the current and pick up whatever tidbit the rushing water could stir up from the bottom of the lake. I was anchored to the side of the main current hoping to intercept marauding pike as they cruised up and down the current break looking for hapless victims. I was rewarded with two fish in the 10-12 lb. Range before the rush of water down the spillway stopped. Travers Reservoir is another large prairie reservoir that is quite unique. Basically a flooded "coulee", it's high sandstone banks and many little bays and fingers of water creates a truly unique place to throw a line. The pike can grow very large here but the trophy fish are more difficult to locate as there is so much water to cover. There are also a fair number of walleye that have been planted and they too can be enticed to take a fly.

Lake Newell

A very large body of water south of the town of Brooks on the #1 Highway east of Calgary. There are many fish in the 30 lb. class in this lake. Could this be the place for a new Alberta Record Pike?

Keho Lake

The current Alberta record pike came out of this lake in 1983 and weighed in at 38 lbs. A popular lake with wind surfers. Head south of Calgary on the #2 Highway to secondary highway and follow the signs.

Cypress Hills

No talk of fishing the prairies is complete without some mention of the lakes of the Cypress Hills. A geological anomaly, the Cypress Hills are a major uplift of land on an otherwise billiard table flat landscape just south east of Medicine Hat. The lakes offer good trout fishing in an almost alpine setting. Well worth a visit.

Alberta's Blue Ribbon Waters

Some of the best waters in the country are found in Alberta. The Bow river is known all over the angling world as one of the best trophy rainbow fisheries. The following is a list of some of the best that can be found in Alberta. Be sure to look at some of the more popular rivers that have been detailed in this book.

West Castle and Castle Rivers

Both of these rivers offer the angler many miles of excellent stream fishing. Highway 774 is the main route into the Castle drainage. Cutthroat, rainbows, bull trout and whitefish can all be found here. Fly fishing is very popular on both rivers. The long slow pools create great cover for trout while the whitefish seem to prefer the ripples. The main access along the Castle is provided by the Castle River Road where stops along the rivers length is a great way to get to know this fine piece of water. Cutthroat are the most predominate but rainbows and bull trout are not uncommon.

Crowsnest Creek

This small creek near Crowsnest Lake is perfect for those who enjoy fishing smaller streams. With many rainbows, cutties and whitefish, it would be tough to have a bad day. These trout are not fussy when it comes to flies and small dries will work well all summer.

Crowsnest River - see detailed chapter

Highwood River

Known as a major tributary of the Bow near Calgary, the Highwood is known to the locals as a great rainbow fishery. Highway 40 parallels the Highwood which makes much of the river easily accessible. Rainbows are most common but other trout can be found. Fly fishing is the preferred method by most anglers on this stream.

Livingstone River - see detailed chapter

Oldman River - see detailed chapter

Dutch Creek

Great fishing over its entire length in this small stream for good sized cutthroat trout. Bull trout and whitefish can also be caught. A variety of tactics can work well.

Kananaskis River

This great stream flows from the Kananaskis lakes to the Bow river and its clear water and deep pools attract plenty of anglers. Brook trout are most common although cutthroat, rainbows, bull trout and whitefish are all present in good numbers. Some anglers are turned off by the possibility of crowds, but the ones who make it usually leave with smiles on their faces.

Bow River - see detailed chapter

Spray River

Joining the Bow river just west of Banff, this fair sized river offers fairly good fishing in both the upper and lower stretches. Cutthroat are found mainly in the upper section while good sized brown trout and rainbows are sought after in the lower waters.

North Ram River - see detailed chapter

Little Smoky River - see detailed chapter

St.Mary River

Runs in and out of the St.Mary Reservoir before joining the Oldman River south west of Lethbridge. Very large pike and whitefish. Some excellent hatches occur through out the year and many opportunities exist for fly fishers. Rainbows exceeding 5 lbs are not uncommon and can be taken on the fly. Catch and release regulations are in place for these trophies downstream from the dam.

Raven River

With large browns and good sized brook trout this fair sized stream can be very rewarding to fish. With all the characteristics of a good brown trout stream, they are the most abundant fish in the river. Streamers can be very effective when fishing the deeper pools and dries in the evenings will also produce some of the larger fish. Watch the regulations carefully. The odd pike and walleye may also be caught in the lower stretches of the river.

South Western Canada
Stream Hatch Chart

NATURAL	IMITATION	TIME
Stone flies		
Tiny Winter Black (Nemoura spp)	Pheasant Tail Nymph (10-16)	March 1 - June 1
Salmon Fly Nymph (Pteronarcys californica)	Brook's Yellow Stone (4-8) Kaufmann's Stone (4-8)	Year Round
Salmon Fly Adult (Pteronarcys californica)	Orange Stimulator (6-8) Sofa Pillow (6-8)	May 15 - June 15
Yellow Sallie (Isoperla spp.)	Gold Ribbed Hare's Ear (8-12) Little Yellow Stone (8-12)	June 1 - August 1
Lime Sallie (Alloperla spp.)	Pheasant Tail Nymph (12-16) Olive Elk Hair Caddis (12-16)	June 15 - September 1
Golden Stone Nymph (Arconeuria pacifica)	Brook's Yellow Stone (6-10) Gold Ribbed Hare's Ear (6-10)	Year Round
Golden Stone Adult (Arconeuria pacifica)	Yellow Stimulator (6-10) Yellow Letort Hopper (6-10)	June 1 - August 1
Caddis flies		
Various Species	Elk Hair Caddis (10-16) Goddard Caddis (10-16)	June 1 - November 1
Great Late-Summer Sedge	Elk Hair Caddis (10-14) (Varied Colors)	August 15 - October 1
October Caddis	Orange Stimulator (8-12) Sofa Pillow (8-12)	August 15 - October 15

NATURAL	IMITATION	TIME

Mayflies

Blue Winged Olive (Baetis spp.)	Pheasant Tail Nymph (10-14) Blue Winged Olive (16-20)	April 15 - October 15
Quill Gordan (Epeorus spp.)	Quill Gordan Dry Fly (12-16) Light Cahill (12-16)	June 1 - August 1
Western Green Drake (Ephemerella grandis)	Green Humpy (8-12) Green Paradrake (8-12)	June 15 - July 15
Small Green Drake (Epheemerella spp.)	Green Humpy (14-18) Green Paradrake (14-18)	July 1 - August 1
March Brown (Rhithrogena morrisoni)	March Brown Dry (12-16) Brown Wolf (12-16)	May 1 - June 15
Pale Morning Dun (Ephemerella infrequens, inermis)	Pale Morning Dun (14-18) Gold Ribbed Hare's Ear (14-18)	June 15 - August 1

Terrestrials

Grasshopper	Joe's Hopper (6-12) Dave's Hopper (6-12)	July 1 - September 15
Ants	Black Ant (12-18) Red Ant (12-18)	July 1 - September 15

Note: Most streams have a variety of these insects and emergence times can vary accordingly.

Safely Releasing Fish

With more waters becoming catch and release every season, everyone needs to be educated in proper procedures. If possible, don't handle the fish. Most fish are covered with a protective slime. When you handle the fish you disturb the slime and the fish can possibly develop fungus in the spots you touch. If using a net try and get one with small enough holes as not to injure fish and cotton is easier on the skin. Do not touch a fish with a dry hand, your hand become abrasive when dry. For small fish I usually just wiggle the hook free and they can easily swim away. Large fish take more time to bring in and require some time to rest up. I like to keep the fish in the net and just hold the tail. The fish will tell you when it's ready to leave.

If you must handle the fish, do so gently by turning the fish on its side or upside down. This usually causes the fish to become immobile. In this position the hook can be removed without any trouble. If I ever have trouble getting a hook out of a fish I just cut the line. These hooks can be shaken out by the fish our they will generally rust out in a few days.

Often I see fish pulled out of the water, squeezed a little, maybe lifted up by the gills, dropped on the boat bottom a few times and finally released. Unfortunately this poor fish has very little chance of surviving. Fish have very delicate parts. The internal organs can be damaged by squeezing and the gills are the same. Large or small it's best to gently hold onto the fish until is swims away. You should be able to see the gills pumping water and if not, it is all right to slowly move the fish back and forth.

In the river the same basics apply. The major difference between lakes and streams is where the fish are released. Never release a large fish in fast water. If you do and the fish is tired, it will roll down stream and you won't be able to catch up to it. I like to release most fish in shallow water where they can immediately lay still and rest. Fish should always be faced upstream when released. Water rushing into their gills backwards can do damage. With catch and release on the rise it's up to us as anglers to see that the fish are properly released.

Some of the great waters in British Columbia

For all East Kootenay lakes please see detailed chapter

Vancouver Island

Campbell River

Better fishing in the spring and fall for rainbows and cutts. Also a good winter run of steelhead and some excellent salmon opportunities.

Cowichan Lake

The headwaters of the Cowichan River and a decent spot to fish for salmon, rainbows, browns, dollies and cutthroat. Nice place to camp and the fishing is usually fair.

Cowichan River

This river seems to get better ever year and that says quite a bit for the stream that may be the best on the island. See detailed chapter by Barry Alldred.

Nanaimo River

Good fishing all season for cutthroat and rainbow but most local anglers spend their time fishing here during the winter run of steelhead after Christmas. Still a good strong stream.

Greater Fraser Valley

Pitt Lake

It's hard to make a list of some of the best spots without mentioning Pitt Lake. This large lake is popular with most anglers and the fishing is great all year. The fish can grow to a good size and everything from rainbows and cutts to sturgeon and steelhead are angled for.

Pitt River

Good fishing on both the upper Pitt and lower although access to the upper Pitt can be a problem if you don't have a boat. This does allow for less pressure on the stream and better fishing always accompanies that. The lower Pitt is more accessible and still great for fishing at times. Check your regs for closures.

Chilliwack River

The fishing has really rebounded here in the last 15 or so years. Very good access for much of its length and a tribute to what proper management can accomplish. Good cutthroat fishing in the spring and fall but most anglers set their sights to the steelhead runs. Check the regs.

Skagit River

Great fly fishing all summer right after run-off for dollies, brookies and nice sized rainbows. One of the most popular streams in the area due to the scenery and quality of trout. A beautiful stream with good access throughout its length.

Greater Interior

Island Lake

Just like many of the famous lakes in B.C., this one is no exception. Large rainbows and catch and release seem to go hand in hand. The lake is restricted to flies only and this seems to be a pretty good idea if you're a fly fisher. Very good hatches all spring with a sedge hatch closer to summer.

Nicola River

A good sized stream that runs from Nicola Lake and offers good fishing for most of its length. Rainbows, dollies, steelhead and salmon can all be caught here if you fish it at the right time.

Douglas Lake Ranch

Part of the renowned Douglas Lake Ranch where you will generally experience good fly fishing for rainbows on these lakes. This is a pay fishery but the money spent can be justified. The ranch contains some of the best lakes in the interior including Stoney, Crater and Minnie plus 9 others. A full service lodge is also available. This is by far the best private fishery anywhere in western Canada. 800-663-4838

Hatheume Lake
This lake has improved lately and now offers some good fishing for the fly fisher. Single barbless hooks and artificial flies only will ensure that this rainbow fishery will survive for a long time. The lake is closed from Dec.1 to April 31 and no winter fishing is allowed.

Kootenay Area- see detailed chapter.

Kamloops Area

Clearwater River
A nice river with some very good fly fishing for rainbows and a few whitefish and dollies as well. Check your regs for special restrictions. Some camping is available. The fishing picks up right after runoff.

Edith Lake
This lake grows trout as fast as anything. There is a good selection of food for both the rainbows and brookies. Before you head out to this lake find out if it has recently winterkilled.

Horseshoe Lake
A productive lake which happens to be very close to Roche Lake. Although the fishing isn't always that good if you hit it right you'll have a great time. Large brook trout are caught every year along with rainbows.

Roche Lake
Great hatches, closed to ice fishing and large rainbows. A fly fishers paradise. It really is one of the most popular lakes in B.C. and it still produces. The fish get pick quickly and if you find the right pattern and fine tippet you'll have a day you'll never forget. Just be prepared to get skunked if you can't find the right pattern! Good camping and a resort as well.

Peterhope Lake

This is one of the more difficult lakes to fish in the area but the reward for success is usually in the form of a large rainbow.

Lac Le Jeune

Located in a large provincial park this lake seems to have very good numbers of fish between 12 and 16 inches along with a few larger ones. A popular lake for anglers of all types and great for the family. A good hatch seems to be always on the go and at times fishing can be easy.

Tunkwa Lake

One of the best chironomid hatches anywhere in B.C. If you want to experience fly fishing a lake for large rainbows, this would be the place. Most anglers concentrate their efforts in the spring and fall, as the summer fishing can be really slow. Attractor patterns can work but the fish spend a great deal of time feeding on plankton.

East Kootenay Highlights

The East Kootenay waters are quickly becoming known as the last best, un-crowded fishing destination. So many of the great waters in the world stand on their own, here in the Kootenays we have many top notch waters and countless others that offer support and spread out any possible fishing pressure. The next few pages will outline some of the best spots around for amazing fishing and spectacular scenery. Don't stop with these streams; explore every spot as almost every puddle in the Kootenays can hold trout.

Streams

Most streams in the Kootenays are filled with an abundant amount of Westslope cutthroat. These fish really are the drawing card to the water. They take the fly with no questions asked and thrive where other trout could not. From the smallest trickles to the great Kootenay River the cutthroat are the most common trout found here. Along with the cutthroat, dollies, rainbows and whitefish are also present and these fish add a nice mix to the water.

Elk River - See detailed chapter

St. Mary - See detailed chapter

Skookumchuck River

This fast flowing stream attracts quite a bit of attention in the summer with some very good fishing for both cutthroat and dollies. The Skookumchuck is perfectly designed for walk and wades and fishing is best after July when the water levels drop. There are always a few bears around and it's not recommended you fish alone. Dry flies work very well all season long as sparse may fly hatches get the fish looking up just about all the time. The Skookumchuck River flows into the Kootenay near the small resort of Skookumchuck. Here you can find a place to stay, a good meal, and many spots to fish within a short drive.

Moyie River

At one time anglers used to troll up the river into Moyie Lake and the fishing was unbeatable. Large rainbows can still be found although access is hard since the ban of motors. Small brook trout, cutthroat and rainbows are plentiful and the hatches are as thick as anywhere else. Carry bug spray and be prepared to do a little bushwhacking as there is not much for access. Below the lake the fishing is always good all the way into the states. A very productive stream with constantly changing character.

Goat River

Since the glory days of past the Goat has seen quite a few changes. The rainbows are mostly small now on the bottom end of the river and the water levels just aren't what they used to be. Still, the fishing can be decent and the cutthroat in the upper end can get to good sizes. Access can be a problem but if you enjoy a good hike and don't mind wading you'll find that the goat is a gem of a stream. Creston offers all the facilities of a small town and the local sports shop can get you set up and headed in the right direction.

Bull River

One of the most popular small streams in the East Kootenays. Camping, fishing, hiking and sightseeing can all be done to the fullest on this gorgeous stream. Most anglers who like fishing from shore will fall in love with this place, the cutthroat take flies greedily and fight well in the cool water. The best time to fish here, along with most of the streams in the Kootenays is after the middle of July. Some years, run-off can cause the water to be high and stained longer than usual.

Little Bull

A quaint small stream close to the hatchery and the Bull River. This creek has an age restriction and is a nice place for kids to spend some quality fishing. The lower end of the stream holds some very large rainbows as the folks at the hatchery do a great job creating the perfect environment. If you get a chance to get into the hatchery it's well worth the time. The Kootenay hatchery is one of the best around and no one can argue with their success.

Lussier River

It could almost be called a creek but the Lussier River can offer some good fly fishing for cutthroat. Even if the fishing were slow the scenery itself would be worth the trip. Just about the entire length of the stream can be good and some anglers spend a lot of time fishing here solely for dollies. Plan on spending some time here if you enjoy fishing the smaller streams.

Wigwam River

As with most tributaries to the Elk River, the Wigwam contains good numbers of large cutthroat. Access is a huge barrier here and I think that's why most people enjoy it. It's not that it's a big secret it's just that most people won't hike an hour through tight bust to catch fish! There are a few access points but usually you will see more people than you like. The Wigwam is just like a large creek and the hatches of mayflies and caddis can be decent. This is one stream I would not walk and wade alone. If you are scared by bears don't even go and if you do go bring along a can of bear spray. Check the regulations before you fish any tributaries of the Elk as some special rules apply.

Lakes

Both big and small lakes can be found in the Kootenays. From Whiteswan to Horseshoe the rainbows that are most common here thrive in the lakes and reach excellent sizes. Most lakes have fish that average 15-16 inches and fish getting over 20 inches is not uncommon at all. Rainbows are stocked into most lakes on a regular basis and the local hatchery has done a superb job with managing our waters. With so many lakes to choose from the following list is just a sample of some of the best and by no means a complete list. Enjoy the water and remember to practice catch and release.

Premier, Whiteswan and Whitetail

"The Big Three" as they are commonly called, attract more anglers than all of the other lakes combined. They are large, deep and cool lakes with good fishing opportunities just about all season long. The fly fishers and trollers both have good success catching these beautiful rainbows and both are rewarded with hard and long fights. The fish here do grow to good sizes with the biggest fish coming from Whiteswan. Whitetail is a true fly fishers lake. Long shoals and huge trout get most guys a little anxious, add in some sight fishing and half of you are already there. Premier offers one thing that the other two lakes don't, brook trout. Not small brooks but long silver bullets, perfect company for the rainbows. Whitetail offers little for camping but the others nearby make up for it. All of these lakes are located off the highway between Cranbrook and Invermere and are posted well.

Alces Lake

Just a short distance from Whiteswan and at times the fishing is comparable. This lake holds decent sized rainbows but is often forgotten due to the incredible fishing at Whiteswan. It's a perfect lake for fly fishing and trolling. The trout can be picky but it's definitely worth a try. A great place to spend the day if the big lake gets a little too windy.

Quartz Lake

This lake has some nice rainbows and gets a fair bit of attention from anglers. Located just next to Premier, many times anglers head here if the fishing gets slow elsewhere. Very similar to Alces in many respects and those that fish here on a regular basis enjoy good success.

Larchwood Lake

Larchwood and Tamarack are two completely different lakes even though they are so close. Larchwood holds a very good number of smaller rainbows that you can catch on just about any thing. This is very popular with families and those who are new to fishing. The camping is better here than Tamarack and Skookumchuck is not that far away.

Tamarack Lake

This lake will give most anglers trouble. Some good sized fish with the occasional trophy but the numbers just aren't that good. The rainbows feed mainly on shiners and fly fishing can be difficult. The plus to this lake is that it neighbor, Larchwood holds all the small fish and a mix of these lakes makes for a nice trout trip.

Horseshoe, Garbutts and Peckams

"The Little Three" located between Cranbrook and the hatchery. Very popular for picnickers and family activities. These lakes are only about 5 minutes apart so if one gets a little slow or crowded you can always move on. The hatchery keeps these lakes stocked all season long with the odd rainbow over 10 lbs. to add a little excitement. For the most part the fishing is easy and enjoyable for everyone.

Northstar Lake

Getting a little closer to Jaffray you'll find some of the nicest lakes around. Both Northstar and Suzanne hold some decent fish but on most days the fishing is slow. Once again rainbows hold in the water and Northstar does have good numbers of smaller fish. Early spring and late fall can be decent if you don't mind the cooler temperatures. The fish aren't too picky and if you hit it on the right day you could have some fun.

Suzanne Lake

This lake can really be frustrating. There are not many fish but if you happen to hook up, chances are good that it's a big one. More large fish are caught (or at least hooked) here each year than all the other lakes together. I think it's fair to say that the fishing is generally slow but if you have patience you might be rewarded. It's not necessarily that the trout get picky but there just aren't that many of them in the lake. I guess if there is a time to fish here it would have to be spring or fall. In the summer months the fish just stay deep and force everyone to troll. Good luck!

Wapiti Lake

There was a time when this lake was full of 5lb footballs. It can still be good but has the tendency to winter-kill. As with many of the lakes in the Jaffray area the rainbows grow big at a top speed. It's a nice lake and worth checking out. Fly fishing will be more popular here and it can be good at all times of the year.

Edwards Lake

The first lake to become ice-free in the spring. Edwards holds some nice rainbows in a variety of sizes and the lake usually fishes its best first thing in spring. This gives most stillwater anglers a chance to hook into a few rainbows before April in some years.

Loon Lake

Right next to Edwards, both these lakes are close to Grasmere and offer some pretty good fishing all year. Both contain rainbows that can reach some good sizes. Camping is available at both lakes. Loon is a smaller lake and doesn't get as much traffic even though the fishing can be as good as anywhere if you hit it right.

Mineral Lake

Both Mineral and Munroe are close to Moyie Lake and traffic can get heavy in the summer months. Most people use these lakes for water sports and the excellent fishing opportunities sometimes go unnoticed. Mineral is smaller than Munroe and the rainbows do not get quite as big here. Fly fishing and trolling can work well in the spring and fall.

Munroe Lake

Every year anglers catch large trout from this lake. In some respects it caters more to the trollers but flies can work well at times. Fish this lake in the spring or fall because the summer crowd will push the trout deep. There aren't as many fish here as mineral but they do tend to get quite a bit larger. Minnow patterns have been known to work better than anything else does.

St.Mary Lake

The headwaters of the St.Mary River. The main reason people enjoy fishing here is because you just never know what you will hook into. Rainbows, cutts, dollies and brook trout all share the lake. If you get tired of fishing the lake you can walk down stream and be fishing the river in just a few minutes. Good fishing for all types of anglers.

New Lake

Just outside Cranbrook and up New Lake road lies a small lake filled with feed and some good sized trout. The only problem may be that there is just too much food offered to the trout. Attractor patterns and leeches seem to work at times but it can be a difficult lake. Best fishing is in spring and fall.

Surveyors Lake

Near the bottom end of the Elk River and in their own camp-ground lies a series of small lakes with the largest being Surveyors. Surveyors' holds some good-sized brook trout to accompany the bass that are in all of the other lakes. Both fly and spin gear can bring in the fish.

Duck Lake

Closer to Creston you will find this large shallow lake that doesn't seem to get deeper than 10 feet at any time. The bottom is covered in dense weed and the bass, perch and sunfish love this place. Very few anglers seem to fish here as bass fishing isn't as popular as trout fishing. If you're looking for a new challenge or just a little fun, spend some time here.

Leach Lake

This is a small lake in behind Duck Lake that has been known to hold some real big bass. In the past it has been known to winterkill but it is definitely worth a try if you're in the area. The bass in both lakes respond well to the spinner and the fly.

Fish Lake

Located in Top of the World Park this small lake is the headwaters to the Lussier River. Although it requires a hike of almost 2 hours the fishing can really be worth it. Many anglers hike up every year and fly fish for both cutthroat and dollies that can reach a good size.

Popular Trout Patterns

Adam's
Adam's, Female
Adam's, Humpy
Adam's, Irresistible
Adam's, Parachute
Adult Damsel
Ant, Black
Ant, Cinnamon
Baetis Sparkle Dun
Baggy Shrimp
Bead Head Caddis Pupa
Bead Head Hare's Ear
Bead Head Leech
Bead Head Pheasant
Bead Head Prince
Bead Head Scud
Beetle, Foam
Bivisible
Black Gnat
Blue Wing Olive
Blue Quill
Bottom Walker
Brassie
Bunny Leech
Caddis, CDC
Caddis, Elk Hair
Caddis Emerger
Caddis, Fluttering
Caddis, Goddard
Caddis, Larva
Caddis, Pupa
Cahill, Dark
Cahill, Light
Cahill, Parachute
Carrey, Special
CDC, Ant

CDC, Comparadun
CDC, Caddis
CDC, Elk Hair
CDC, Emerger
CDC, Emerging Nymph
CDC, Floating Nymph
Chernobly Ant
Chironomids, All colors
Clouser Minnow
Coachman
Damsel, Marabou
Dave's Hopper
Doc Spratley
Dragon Nymphs
Dun, Olive
Dun, Blue
Dun, Brown
Egg Sucking Leech
Extended Body Mayfly
Flashback Hare's Ear
Flashback Pheasant Tail
Floating Nymph, Blue-Winged Olive
Floating Nymph, Pale Morning Dun
Floating Nymph, Slate Tan
Fluttering Stone
Flying Ant, Black
Flying Ant, Cinnamon
Foam Ant
Freshwater Shrimp, Black
Freshwater Shrimp, Olive
Freshwater Shrimp, Pink
Glass Bead Midge, All colors
Gold Ribbed Hare's Ear
Green Drake
Green Drake, Extended
Green Drake, Parachute
Griffith's Gnat
Grizzly Midge
Grizzly Wulff

H + L Varient
Half Back, All colors
Hare's Ear, All colors
Hendrickson
Henry's Fork Hopper
Humpy, All colors
Interior Sedge
Janssen's Minnow, Brook
Janssen's Minnow, Rainbow
Joe's Hopper
Kamloops Pupae
Knouff Lake Special
Krystal Bugger, All colors
Lady McConnel
Leech, Marabou, All colors
Leech, Mohair, All colors
Madame X
March Brown, Dry
March Brown, Nymph
Marabou Muddler
Matuka, All colors
Mayfly, Blue Winged Olive
Mayfly, Pale Morning Dun
Mickey Finn
Midge, CDC
Midge, Peacock
Mini Leech, All colors
Mironymph, All colors
Montana Stone
Mosquito
Muddler Minnow
Mysis Shrimp
No-Hackle, All colors
October Caddis
Pale Morning Dun, Dry
Pale Morning Dun, Emerger
Pale Morning Dun, Floating
Parachute Ant
Parachute, Dun
Paradrake, Brown
Paradrake, Green

Peacock Caddis
Peeking Caddis, All colors
Pheasant Tail
Prince Nymph
Prince Nymph, Bead Head
Quill Gordon, Dry
Quill Gordon, Nymph
Renegade
Royal Coachman
Royal Humpy
Royal Stimulator
Royal Wulff
Rubber Legs
Salmon fly, Henry's Fork
San Juan Worm
Sculpin, All colors
Serendipity, All colors
Slow Water Caddis, All colors
Sofa Pillow
Sparkle Dun, All colors
Spinner, CDC
Spinner, Poly Yarn
Stimulator, All colors
Stone, Black
Stone, Brown
Stone, Golden
Ted's Stone
Telico
Thorax, All colors
Tom Thumb
Trico, Dun
Trico, Poly Spinner
Water Boatman
White Wulff
Woolly Bugger, All colors
Woolly Bugger, Bead Head
Woolly Worm, All colors
Zonker, All colors
Zug Bug
Zug Bug, Bead Head

Popular Steelhead Patterns

Steelhead Flies
Air B.C.
Babine Special
Black Boss
Bomber
Egg Sucking Leech
Fall Favorite
Freight Train
General Practitioner
Glow Bug, Pink
Glow Bug, Orange
Goddard Sedge
Greased Liner
Juicy Bug
Muddler Minnow
Muddler Minnow, Rolled
October Caddis
Patrica
Patriot
Polar Shrimp
Purple Peril
Royal Humpy
Royal Wulff
Silver Hilton
Skunk
Steelhead Bee
Steelhead Caddis
Thor
Umpqua Special
Undertaker

Popular Salmon Patterns

Blue Zonker
Bright Roe
Coho Blue Minnow
Coho Rolled Minnow
Fall Favorite
Glow Bug
Green Wienie
Mickey Finn
Moose's Ugly
Orange Boss
Rusty Rat
Silver Rat
Spade
The Pink Fly